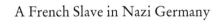

A French Slave in Nazi Germany

A FRENCH SLAVE
IN NAZI GERMANY

A TESTIMONY

ELIE POULARD

Translated and edited by Jean V. Poulard

UNIVERSITY OF NOTRE DAME PRESS | NOTRE DAME, INDIANA

University of Notre Dame Press
Notre Dame, Indiana 46556
www.undpress.nd.edu

Names: Poulard, Elie, 1921– | Poulard, Jean V. (Jean Victor), 1939– translator.
Title: A French slave in Nazi Germany : a testimony /
Elie Poulard ; translated and edited by Jean V. Poulard.
Other titles: Mâemoires d'un Jociste dâeportâe du travail. English
Description: Notre Dame, Indiana : University of Notre Dame Press, [2016] |
Includes bibliographical references.
Identifiers: LCCN 2016023972 (print) | LCCN 2016026827 (ebook) |
ISBN 9780268100773 (hardcover : alk. paper) | ISBN 0268100772 (hardcover :
alk. paper) | ISBN 9780268100797 (pdf) | ISBN 9780268100803 (epub)
Subjects: LCSH: Poulard, Elie, 1921– | France. Service du travail
obligatoire—Biography. | World War, 1939–1945—Conscript labor—
Germany. | Jeunesse ouvriáere chrâetienne (France)—Biography. |
World War, 1939–1945--Deportations from France.
Classification: LCC D805.G3 P67813 2016 (print) |
LCC D805.G3 (ebook) | DDC
940.54/05 [B] —dc23
LC record available at https://lccn.loc.gov/2016023972

To our three sisters,
Jeanne, Rolande, Micheline,
and their families;
and in memory of our brother Roger.

Contents

List of Illustrations – ix

Author's Preface – xi

Acknowledgments – xvii

Editor's Introduction – xix

CHAPTER 1
Still Free: The Phony War – 1

CHAPTER 2
The Real War and the Exodus – 7

CHAPTER 3
Back Home under German Occupation – 15

CHAPTER 4
In Bondage: Forced Labor in the Todt Organization – 19

CHAPTER 5
Deported to Germany – 27

CHAPTER 6
Work at the Möhnetal Dam – 34

CHAPTER 7
Living Conditions at the Dam – 43

CHAPTER 8
Hagen-in-Westfalen and Its Camps – 49

CHAPTER 9
Work at the *Telegraphenamt* of Hagen – 57

CHAPTER 10
Life at the Boeler Heide Camp – 66

CHAPTER 11
Dortmund-South Work Site – 72

CHAPTER 12
Dortmund *Hauptbahnof* after October 6, 1944 – 77

CHAPTER 13
The Ruhr under the Bombs – 85

CHAPTER 14
On the Ruhr: Hengsteysee and Herdecke – 90

CHAPTER 15
In Railroad Yards Still and Again – 97

CHAPTER 16
My Last Week as a Slave – 107

CHAPTER 17
Peace and Return to Mareuil-sur-Aÿ – 116

Epilogue – 123

Appendix: A Dispute over a Title – 128

Notes – 133

Bibliography – 141

Illustrations

All images are from the translator's private collection.

Elie in 1936, an apprentice assistant pharmacist – xii

The Mareuil municipal band at La Villa d'Aÿ, a suburb of Epernay, June 10, 1934 – xiii

Elie and his saxophone, 1938 – 4

Elie, pharmacist – 12

Solange, Elie, and Jeanne in Saint-Honoré-les-Bains, 1940 – 13

Jeanne, Elie, and Jacqueline in Saint-Honoré-les-Bains, 1940 – 13

Elie in 1942 – 20

Pages from the *Jociste* Missal Elie stepped on – 87

Elie's repatriation card – 119

Elie and his wife, Solange, at a *Gasthof* behind the Möhnetal Dam, June 5, 2002 – 122

Elie in front of the Möhnetal Dam, June 5, 2002 – 122

Author's Preface

To add my testimony to history and for my children and grandchildren to remember, here is the story of what I lived through during the Second World War, and how I felt about the events that marked those six horrible years.

I spent my youth and my adolescence in the village of Mareuil-sur-Aÿ in the middle of the valley of the river Marne, which gave its name to two ghastly battles during the First World War. Like all the young men and women of that region, I was deeply affected by the view of the ruins and the numerous military cemeteries left behind by that war. I was obsessed with the idea that those of my generation might have to witness also such horrors. With the rise of Hitler in Germany and the advent of the Nazi regime, my fears increased, and I thought that, unless a miracle happened, nothing could stop a new impending catastrophe. Yet if the politicians that governed France had been a bit more clear-sighted, it could have been averted.

Beginning in April 1934, I was employed by the Clerc pharmacy, located in the town of Aÿ, as an apprentice to become an assistant pharmacist. I remember that as I arrived at the establishment on March 7, 1936, a *gendarme*[1] at the counter was commenting on the day's event: the reoccupation of the demilitarized region of the Rhineland by German troops. This was a clear violation of the Treaty of Versailles, which had ended World War I. This policeman was arguing that the only valid response was to send the French army into that territory to push back Hitler's move and that it could be done without too much bloodshed. If that was not done, he predicted, France would be at war in three or four years. I thought the man was right, and I believed that many other people were in favor of French action. The *gendarme* had indeed sized up the situation correctly.

Hitler had made his first move on the chessboard of Europe. Since there was no reaction from the French or the British, he was comforted in his intentions. Two years later, on March 12, 1938, he annexed Austria to the Third Reich in what was called the *Anschluss*.

Elie in 1936, an apprentice assistant pharmacist.

—✦— After leaving school at the age of twelve, having passed my *Certificat d'Etudes*,[2] I began to learn music. I took saxophone lessons for four months, and at the beginning of April 1934, I became a member of the Mareuil-sur-Aÿ *fanfare*, or municipal band. In June 1938, I successfully passed the exam of the first section of the Confédération Musicale de France. In doing so, I received a first prize in *solfège*[3] and in saxophone with twenty points out of twenty. The jury was composed of Monsieur Petit, who was president of the Musical Federation of Champagne and Meuse, and Monsieur Jules Moineaux from the village of Chouilly. The latter was the assistant director of the Grande Fanfare Champenoise. This great regional band was then led by Félicien Foret, who was assistant director of the Paris Republican Guard's brass band.[4]

The Grande Fanfare was a high level orchestra. To become a member of it, one had to have excellent references or be sponsored by a current member. In my case, I was presented by Monsieur Moineaux, who had highly recommended that I be part of that orchestra after I had done so well on the musical exam mentioned above. Thus, I had the honor to play in that orchestra for a year.

At that time, a young man from Mareuil, Marcel Braine, had organized a group of Jeunesses Ouvrières Catholiques (JOC), or

The Mareuil municipal band at La Villa d'Aÿ, a suburb of Epernay, June 10, 1934.

Catholic Working Youth, an organization formed to keep young people religiously involved after they had joined the work force. I joined the group along with some of my friends. We would meet once a week, and, once a month, we would invite other young men of the town to join us as our guests. Once the Germans occupied Mareuil in 1940, these meetings were forbidden. However, I remained faithful to the JOC, and this organization had a great influence on my entire life.

— In September 1938, the French government mobilized its military reservists, those who had been given a so-called *fascicule bleu*—a blue military booklet. Among them were men who had already fought in World War I, such as Mareuil's mandoline teacher, Monsieur Gotrot. I remember that these men left with the intention of bringing Hitler down. They said that they preferred to fight again so that their sons would not know the horrors of war. Unfortunately, instead of a fight there was the shame of the September 29, 1938, accords of Munich, which gave to Hitler a good chunk of Czechoslovakia. Faced with foolish Western leaders, he invaded the rest of that country on March 15, 1939. Still, most people around me wanted to believe in Hitler's promise of peace. Alas!

On April 30, 1939, the Grande Fanfare gave its annual concert, broadcast on the radio, from the theater of Epernay. This concert was honored by the presence of Henri Rabaud, member of the French Academy and director of the National Conservatory of Paris. During the reception, Monsieur Moineaux introduced me to the music director of the 106th Infantry Regiment of Reims, because I wanted to enlist in the army musical corps so that I could be involved in musical studies. I wanted to make music my profession. It was decided that I would meet him some day at the military band quarters, and that he would accompany me to have my physical examination.

By that time, I had finished my apprenticeship and was thus an assistant pharmacist. Monsieur Clerc had sold his establishment to Jeanne Pierson, a young pharmacist with a diploma from the University of Nancy; Monsieur Clerc's former assistant had another job in the Paris region. Thus I replaced him, though with a much lower salary. But then, I did not really want to make a career as an assistant pharmacist.

In June 1939, I passed my second musical exam, at a higher level, of the Musical Confederation of France. Again, I obtained first prize in *solfège* and musical dictation with twenty points out of twenty. I also got first prize with my saxophone with a grade of 19.5 and the congratulations of the jury for my performance.

Near the end of June, I went to the *caserne*, an urban military base, of the 106th Infantry Regiment. There, I asked for the music director, but unfortunately I was told that he was off that day. However, I found a warrant officer who directed the saxophones. To my surprise, this fellow was the man who had played next to me in the Grande Fanfare. With him was a certain Dervaux, the son of a piano teacher from Aÿ. They made me play my instrument as a test, and they concluded that I would not have any problem being incorporated into the army musical corps. Thus, I went to the infirmary to take my physical. A young doctor examined me and found that I was fit to serve.

His superior, however, arrived before I had left and examined me in his turn. He found that I was too skinny, and nullified the decision of his subordinate. I was very disappointed but decided to come back one day to try again to meet the music director. But I put off my visit too long, and soon the end of August arrived. Considering the unfolding events, I gave up on my project of getting into the 106th Infantry Regiment. Then, my life, just like that of so many other people, was drastically affected by the German aggression and occupation of my home town.

Acknowledgments

The translation of all French sources cited in this little book is my own. However, there were instances where good English equivalents could not be found, such as the term *Déportés du Travail*. Thus, I have left the words in French while providing further explanations in the endnotes. The translation of German phrases are also my own.

I want to thank my wife, Regina, for proofreading the early manuscript, and especially my young colleague, Associate Professor of History Christopher Young of Indiana University Northwest, for making so many suggestions and editing some of my sentences. William Benjamin Radell, Instructional Technology Consultant at I.U.N., also deserves a big thank you for so expertly and efficiently transcribing my files from one word processing program to another.

I want to particularly mention Herr Dieter Tillmann, who has been on several projects of mine a most valuable collaborator and investigator, and encouraged the writing of this book.

Finally, I am very grateful for the support given to this work by Dr. Stephen Little, my University of Notre Dame Press editor, for his publishing guidance. I want to particularly thank Matthew Dowd, my copy editor, for his exceptional work on the manuscript and whose suggestions have been invaluable.

Jean V. Poulard
Michiana Shores,
February 2016

Editor's Introduction

What follows are the recollections of one of the 600,000 Frenchmen who were sent against their will to work for the German Nazi regime by the French government. Such was the fate of Elie Poulard, a very religious young man, twenty-two-years old in 1943, forced into hard labor by an ignominious "law" of the French Vichy government called Service du Travail Obligatoire, or STO for short.[1] After their liberation, these unfortunate young men were often treated in France with suspicion, not to say as collaborators.

In 1939, when World War II began in Europe, Elie had not been conscripted into the French army, for he was only eighteen. By the time he would have been drafted, France had lost the war, and the Germans occupied most of the country, including the village where he lived with his family, on the Marne River in the heart of the Champagne country. When he left for forced labor in Germany, I, his youngest brother, was about three years old. When he was liberated in 1945 by the Americans and came home, I barely knew him. It took me a long time to look upon him as my big brother, especially since he soon left home to settle in the Nièvre department in central France, where he was born.

It was not until the 1960s that we began to see each other regularly. It was when we were alone, sometimes late at night, that we would have long discussions that turned to his experiences during the war. He would tell me stories about his life in Germany, mentioning the places he had been sent to, names of many of the people he had met, and describing his hard labor in different work sites.

He had suffered greatly during his two years as not much more than a slave of the Nazi regime. However, he was not bitter; he always inserted some humor in his descriptions. As a fervent Catholic, he considered that what he had endured was the will of God and a test of his faith.

Thus, for the better part of thirty years, I heard him retelling his anecdotes, very often prodded by my questions: Why did he not join the Résistance? Why did he not just go into hiding? Did anyone try to help him do that? Did he meet decent Germans along the way? Who mistreated him the most? What horrors had he seen? I was always asking for as many details as he could give. One day, I finally asked my brother to put down on paper all of these stories, all these recollections, and to send his handwritten pages to me. I said that I would type and edit them, organize them into chapters, and ultimately send him a manuscript that he could perhaps get published in France. It was only in 1994 that he began to write his recollections of the awful time he had spent in Germany.

By 1996, we had a decent manuscript in French that had been reviewed by several of our friends. Attempts to get it published by one French university press or another were unsuccessful. However in 2005, four hundred copies were printed as a small booklet by the Association Départementale des Déportés du Travail de la Nièvre,[2] to which Elie belonged. Rather than using the somewhat bland title that I had given it, *Témoignages de Guerre,* or *War Testimonies,* Elie chose a longer title that made the point that he had not merely been an unwilling slave of the Nazis, but rather, as a devout Catholic and member of the Jeunesse Ouvrière Catholique (JOC),[3] he had done his bit to resist his masters, especially with his spiritual assistance to his comrades, something strictly forbidden by the Nazis. Thus, he entitled his book *Mémoires d'un Jociste Déporté du Travail: Résistance Spirituelle, 1943–1945.*

This little book was well received by those who bought and read it. (See for example, the letter to Elie written by Monsignor Charles Mollette, translated in the epilogue). A second, more limited edition was printed with a few additions and a better binding. It is that edition, with some minor alterations, that I have translated and edited here.

In the literature on World War II, not much appears about the use of foreign workers by the Nazi regime or their fate, especially in English, but also in French. However, one book, *Vichy France: Old Guard and New Order, 1940–1944*, deals to some extent with the subject. Although the book is mostly about the politics of the Vichy regime under Marshall Pétain and its negotiations with the Nazi regime, the author, Robert Paxton, describes in some length the French government's willing collaboration in providing Germany with French manpower. Paxton provides the following statistics: "By November 1943, 1,344,000 French males were working in German factories, slightly ahead of the Russian and Polish male contingents." French women amounted to 44,000.[4]

In the introduction to the second edition of his book, in its French version, Paxton reiterates the point that "France became the principal foreign supplier of manpower, raw materials and manufactured goods for the German war machine."[5] A few pages later, he reemphasizes the point: "Of all the occupied western countries, it was France that supplied to the German factories the greatest number of workers."[6] What the book does not go into is the fate of these people and their suffering, especially those who were sent to Germany under the Service du Travail Obligatoire law. Paxton simply says: "The German government spared Frenchmen none of the agonies of forced labor."[7] It is on this point that Elie's memoirs fill the gap.

As will be discussed further in the appendix, the French have on the whole been rather ambivalent in dealing with this important episode of the Vichy government's collaboration with the Germans. Even the former STOs themselves are often reluctant to discuss their experiences, as the journalist Jean-Pierre Vittori says at the beginning of his book *Eux, Les S.T.O.*:

> Often, they speak about their past with a certain embarrassment. They tell you: "I was STO," as if they were admitting they had a contagious disease. This is because, in contrast to the former members of the *Résistance*, they do not measure up; these men . . . periodically faced the accusation: Didn't they

work for Nazi Germany? Thus, when people who are not of their generation but want to know about their history and take the time to listen to them, they are astonished.[8]

When it comes to the studies of the STO, Vittori adds: "C'est le vide."[9] Beyond one great exception that Vittori mentions, there is nothing. Researchers from the universities are not interested. Whatever stories and documents are published on the subject are done at the expense of the authors. These works reveal facts that many in France prefer left untold. One of these is the little book of Roger Jaillot, *Le Bal de la Classe*, about a raid by the SS in Decize on February 6, 1944, on a banquet and a dance organized to celebrate the twentieth birthday of about fifty of those who would have been conscripted in normal circumstances.[10] The women who participated in this dance were let go, but the young men were rounded up and sent to work in Germany. In that case, as in others, the French authorities often manipulated the figures, counting some of them as volunteers to work in Germany. Vittori, in his investigation of this affair from Decize, devotes several pages of his book to it and concludes: "The pseudo-volunteers from Decize maintain that they never signed any contracts. Were they signed for them?"[11] The answer to this question is undoubtedly yes.

Vittori's book does not neglect to refer to the fate of Christians attempting to live their faith. In the summer of 1943, the Nazi regime made it a crime for STOs to exercise their religion and for priests among them to say mass. It was in December 1943 that a systematic hunt of Catholics commenced. The Nazis were looking particularly for priests and seminarists who had come to Germany in the disguise of civil workers. JOC groups that had formed in the STO camps were to be dissolved. Those caught faced being sent to a prison or, worse, to a concentration camp.[12]

Vittori's book is indeed an important journalistic investigation of the deportation of French workers to forced labor in Nazi Germany. The goal, as its author declared, was to find *la vérité vraie*.[13] Indeed this book achieved its goal. Still, it did not provide the kind of testimony of the STOs' suffering as Elie's memoirs do.

—✦— The only real academic study of the STO, the exception Vittori mentions, is that of Jacques Evrard, *La Déportation des Travail-*

leurs Français dans le IIIe Reich, which was published in 1972. The author of this rather monumental work was a professor of literature at the lycée Bellevue of Toulouse, was himself a victim of the STO law, and spent two years at forced labor in Germany. When he started to do his research, he asked for some testimonies from former STOs. Those who responded to his request amounted to 152. Although their testimonies are not always footnoted, they are all listed at the end of the book's bibliography, including my brother, Elie.

Evrard's study has become the reference book of the deportation of French workers to Germany during World War II. The paucity of works on this subject was what spurred his research. As Evrard puts it in his foreword:

> In France . . . if, after the collapse of Germany, at the time of investigations of war crimes, official bodies have mentioned the phases of requisitions of manpower; if several former *déportés du travail* have published their memories, no overall study has been devoted to their living conditions in the Third Reich. The present work, which—needless to say—does not pretend to be either complete nor especially definitive, tries to make up for this lacuna.[14]

The book not only offers a history of the Vichy government's deportation of French workers to Germany, especially under its prime minister Pierre Laval, it also goes into great detail about the work and the living conditions of the STOs. It describes all the difficulties that these young men faced from hunger and the lack of proper clothing during the harsh winters or for protection in the handling of certain dangerous products and the brutality of some of their overseers.

Many of the testimonies from STOs that are included in the book show that, more often than not, these captive workers were given tasks that were beyond their strength. Some of these young men were in fact worked to death. Here are a couple of examples Evrard provides:

> At I. G. Farben, in Bitterfeld, because those who repaired the machines producing chlorine were not provided with masks,

they frequently suffered inflammation of the lungs and even of asphyxiation. But, a worker declares, "we did not dare to protest, because we always feared the disciplinary camp." At the freight station of Innsbruck, Lucien Andréani had to unload from the railroad cars animals that had died during their too long journey, and, in Munich, Pierre Mas, employed by a recuperator of bones, collected dead animals destined for . . . the Maggi plants.[15]

This important work thus presents another ugly side of the Nazi regime besides the horrors perpetrated in the concentration camps.

In his conclusion, Evrard discusses the quarrel over the use of the word *déporté*, and the ambiguous status of the STOs in French society. He says:

> Everything considered, this distressing quarrel around a word (a word that twenty-five years later involves the honor of one or another), it is on September 4, 1942, that it was born. The victims of the S.T.O. would have never been suspected to have consented, or half consented, to let themselves be sent to Germany if it were not for a French law, promulgated by the French government and entrusted for its execution to the French bureaucracy that subjugated them.[16]

Since the law was the work of Pétain's prime minister Laval, a man convinced that collaboration with the Germans was in the interest of France and thus was willing to furnish them with French manpower, Evrard states that his "fault was terribly grave and his responsibility damning."[17]

It is interesting to note that Evrard's book was never translated into English. The subject does not seem to interest either English or American academics. The reason, it can be ventured, is perhaps that neither Englishmen nor Americans were subjected to forced labor in Germany during World War II. Whatever the case may be, I hope that this book might be a valuable addition to the English and American literature on World War II.

CHAPTER 1

Still Free
The Phony War

September 1, 1939: The German army invades Poland.

September 3, 1939: Great Britain and France declare war on Germany and order the general mobilization of their armed forces. That Sunday morning, at the Saint Hilaire church of Mareuil, the eighty-four-year-old priest, Father Schmitt, ended his sermon with these prophetic words: "Justice will triumph!"

The days that followed were spent with anxiety about what would happen next. I remember having asked my father, a veteran of World War I: "How long will it take for the German planes to come to us? Will we be warned? Will we have the time to seek shelter?" For us, the shelters were the Champagne cellars. And there was also the fear that gas might be used. Since nobody had a gas mask, everyone looked for a way to get protection. One way was to use crystals of thiosulphate soda. The sale of this product in the pharmacies set a record.

The Champagne region was located in the "zone of the armies" or "war zone." In the first days after the mobilization, cities and villages were transformed into garrison towns. As far as Mareuil was

1

concerned, the Sixth Engineer Regiment from Angers, that is, approximately three thousand soldiers, invaded the village. At the west entrance of the village, in the direction of Aÿ, there was a mansion that had been the property of a lady by the name of Madame Etienne, but the mansion was known as the "chateau Gossard," after the name of its original owner. Because it was unoccupied since the death of its owner, the British Royal Air Force had installed in it a military hospital. Among the soldiers billeted there was an interpreter who spoke French extremely well. On the whole, however, the people of Mareuil did not have much contact with these men. For a while, in the town of Aÿ, the British had installed anti-aircraft batteries in the park close to the canal.

The Royal Canadian Air Force occupied an air base on the south side of Mareuil, where the flat and vast plain of Châlons begins, on the right bank of the Marne River between the villages of Oiry and Plivot. Its planes were Hurricane fighters, which had one wing painted white and the other black. I remember that, a few years before the war, I had witnessed the work of bulldozers that prepared the tarmac. Bizarre coincidence, no?

Most people, including me, had faith in the final victory of the Allies over the Nazis. In the first days of the war, we were told that French troops had entered the Saar. And then, there was the impregnable Maginot line! This was true. But the Germans never really attacked it. Its major defect was that it did not go far enough to protect the frontier, for it stopped near the forest of the Ardennes. This fortress was occupied by special regiments that were relieved often enough, for the men in it, after a certain time, became affected by claustrophobia. Since 1938, to lengthen the Maginot line, fortified blockhouses had been built to stretch all the way to the North Sea. But rumors said that some were not deep enough for the recoil of cannons. Was it true? What is certain is the fact that there was quite a bit of sabotage done and that the French system of defense was muddled.

Posters plastered on walls proclaimed: "We will win because we are the stronger." Other posters called for the donation of scrap metal to forge the "victorious steel." The chief of the allied forces was a French general, General Gamelin. His claim to fame was that his name was given to the hole in which each soldier would seek refuge when attacked. He turned out to be an incompetent leader. At the beginning of the hostilities, the Allies organized the blockade of Germany, on the ground and at sea, hoping to keep it from obtaining raw materials and food, thereby shortening the war. They had not foreseen that the Soviets would provide aid to Hitler. They furnished him with oil and other raw materials. The Germans also made synthetic fuel out of coal.

After a few weeks, as nothing was taking place, the French population settled itself into what became known as the "phony war." In the region where I lived, the villages had two or three times more soldiers than civilians, and many contacts took place between them and the civil population, especially the young. With my friends, I would go out on Sundays in the company of several soldiers. Those that were closest to us were from Picardie, a region north of the region of Champagne. They spoke with a sort of old French that amused us. Sometimes, they would confide in us their anxiety about what might come next. They would mention much disorder in their military units. For example, they told us that the guards of their camps did not have any bullets in their rifles. One day, one told us in his Picard way: "If the Germans send parachutists, they will do what they want." These soldiers also told us about the incompetence of their officers. They respected only one, a captain by the name of Leclerc.

I got acquainted with a few musicians who had been members of the regiment's band. Because the band had been dissolved at the beginning of the war, they were idle, but they had their musical instruments. I asked my parents their permission to invite these men to our house to make music. My mother responded by saying that it would keep my baby brother Jean from falling asleep. I ended up by convincing her that the music would in fact rock him to sleep.

Thus, one evening a week, we would be in my house to make music. We really were a small orchestra. We worked on the orchestration of small classics from the Salabert editions to which I subscribed. There was a flutist, Raymond Marandy from Bordeaux, who had received a prize from the music conservatory, a clarinettist, Claverie, and a tuba player whose name I have forgotten. My sisters, Jeanne and Rolande, would play their mandolines, and I would play the part of the cello with my saxophone. We had a lot of fun making music, and my little brother would sleep like a dormouse.

Elie and his saxophone, 1938.

The village was without a priest after the death of Father Schmitt on October 21, 1939. An army chaplain would say mass for the parish. A group of youth formed a choir that I directed, and, some Sundays, Raymond Marandy played his flute during mass. He interpreted for us, among other pieces, the famous *Meditation* from the opera *Thais* of Jules Massenet. There was also a young opera singer, Renée Sorgue, who was at her grandparents' in Mareuil. She would sometimes sing solo, accompanied by Monique Philipponnat at the harmonium. Unfortunately, Renée died of tuberculosis at the age of twenty, at the beginning of the German occupation.

My sisters, Jeanne, Rolande, and Micheline, were taking piano lessons from Monsieur Carteret, professor of music in Epernay. I got to know him before the war when I was a member of the Epernay municipal choir of which he was the director. Beside the piano, Jeanne practiced the harmonium so she could play at funerals during the week. She would practice every day during the noon hour, playing over and over again the "joyful" portions of the mass for the dead! During that time, I practiced playing my saxophone in my room on the second floor of the house.

Before the war, I was also a member of a jazz orchestra in Epernay. The name of that orchestra was "Patro Jazz" because it was associated with the Catholic *patronage*, or youth club.[1] At the trumpet there was Jean Houlmont, at the drums, his brother, Roger. There was also an accordionist and a pianist, but I have forgotten their names. We gave performances at the movie theater of the *patronage*, which had 1200 seats and a large stage comparable to that of a normal theater. We played as well in church fairs in the region, and we had the occasion to play at dances. At the beginning of the war, we stopped our activities when a British infantry regiment established its quarters inside the *patronage*. However, after some weeks, Jean Houlmont, who lived on the same street, managed to come in contact with some officers and got permission for our orchestra to continue to make music in our usual place. We then resumed our rehearsals. We played our full repertoire of classic jazz, which the soldiers appreciated with enthusiasm. One of them, whose name was Jeff Craven, played the piano without ever having learned the rudiments of music. I remember that he would interpret *The Swan* of Saint-Saëns to perfection. We had the occasion to perform the background music during performances of their theater of the armies. The theater of the *patronage* was full of soldiers, and much beer was consumed. We also played several Sundays at the French Soldiers Club of Epernay with an authentic Tyrolian singer, Debau. He was, I believe, one of the rare French Tyrolian singers. He had cut several records. As a cellar man by profession, he was employed by the Champagne firm Moët et Chandon. In Epernay, there was also, among others, a regiment composed of hotheads who were called *Les Joyeux*, the "Merry Men." They were responsible for numerous fights in the cafés of the city, which caused quite a bit of damage.

During this period, a radio show in French was broadcast from Stuttgart, starring a man by the name of Fredonnet, who was called in France "the traitor of Stuttgart." Oddly, he was well informed about all that took place in the "zone of the armies." He would give us news about our own region. That proved that the German intelligence services were well organized. There was the famous "fifth column,"[2] which was going to win fame from May to June 1940. On this score, in Mareuil, in the rue d'Avenay, at the end of the village, there was a house in which a supposedly retired Norwegian consul and his wife and daughter lived. The latter was so skinny that the girls of Mareuil called her "fine needle." After the attack of the village on May 10, 1940, men from the Passive Defense alleged that they had seen him giving signals to German planes. These men took justice in their own hands and killed him on the spot. In Aÿ, there was also a manufacturer of *paillons*,[3] who made himself pass for a Luxemburger. He had been several times convicted of indecent acts, and I believe even of pedophilia. One day, he was deported from France. However, we saw him again as a Lieutenant of the Wehrmacht!

The winter of 1939–40 was harsh and long. The temperature went down to minus five Fahrenheit, and with this intense cold there was much snow. The canal was frozen over, as were ponds left by floods from the Marne River in the plain of Oiry. This made for beautiful skating rinks, and we all enjoyed them. During the whole winter, a barge was moored in the port of Mareuil. It was transformed into a movie theater. That gave us some entertainment on Sundays when we were not going to a movie in Epernay. We were still the same band of friends, but Hubert Remy was missing, for he had been mobilized.

In April 1940, Monsieur Foret convened the Grande Fanfare Champenoise for an informational meeting, which he concluded with these words: "If nothing happens before the end of the month of May, we can suppose that the war will end, as will the effects of the blockade. Then, we will be able to have our rehearsals again." Well, the man was fantasizing!

One evening near the end of April, after sunset, we heard the noise of an airplane motor, a sort of wailing, similar to the sound of a siren. We rushed to the door of the house. The sky was illuminated by the light of a great fire. It was from a German plane that had gone down in flames. It fell into a park at the entrance of Avenay, and the whole crew was killed. Of course, my father and I went running in the direction of the crash, but we were not able to get close. Many soldiers ran with us, and I remember a somewhat comical detail. One soldier, with a strong Mediterranean accent, told another: "If I flinch, you will support me, no?" This was our first taste of the real war.

CHAPTER 2

The Real War and
the Exodus

On May 1, I started an unskilled job in the De Ayala Champagne firm of Aÿ. I took the job because I would earn double what I was getting as an assistant pharmacist. Also, I was thinking that it would not be long before my class[1] was mobilized. The work was hard, and the difference in temperature between the underground cellars and outside, where it was very warm, did not take long to make me sick. Thus, I worked there barely two weeks.

During the night of May 9 and 10, I was sick; I had problems with my adenoids. Near midnight, I got up because I was nauseous. That woke up my father, who also got up. At that moment, we heard the humming of motors. We went down to the landing of the kitchen door. Once outside, we became aware that the noise came from planes, and there were many. We went back to bed, but, on the morning of May 10, I was suddenly awakened by the noise of motors and machine-gun fire from airplanes. At that moment we became aware that the German attack had started and that the real war had begun. During the days that followed, we did not worry too much; our confidence in the Allied armies was unshakable. But later, we were inundated by long and compact lines of people that were evacuating the Ardennes and by convoys of troops going in the opposite direction toward Belgium. Soon, an office of the Liaudet Enterprise, abutting our house, became a depot of explosives, and soldiers loaded them unto trucks to bring them to the front. There was always a truck in front of our house fully loaded with enough explosives to blow up a good portion of the village.

The following Monday, the day after Pentecost, along with Monsieur Gotrot, his son Loulou, and my sisters Jeanne and Rolande, I went out to pick lilies of the valley in the forest of Reims above Louvois. As we were walking, we were surprised by low-flying airplanes, and we sought refuge in the ditch alongside the road. However, this did not stop us, and we continued our outing. During all the time we spent in the forest, we heard the noise of the carousel of planes above Reims and of the anti-aircraft guns. During that week, we continued to live as usual. From time to time, we witnessed planes passing by and occasional aerial fights. Often, we watched the take-off of British Hurricanes. The traitor Fredonnet at the Stuttgart radio regularly mentioned the names of bombed cities and would announce to us the bombing of Mareuil. We did not want to believe him, but on the morning of Sunday, May 19, it was our turn. I was getting ready to go to mass when Stukas arrived above Mareuil. We all went down into the cellar under our house. The first wave dove on a *paillon* factory between Mareuil and Aÿ, some one-third of a mile from our house. These planes were equipped with a siren and their bombs with whistles. All that made such a terrifying noise that it led to some panic in part of the village's population, but not everywhere. That morning, my brother Roger was at the barber,[2] whose customers, including him, went out on the street to look calmly at the spectacle.

The same day, around two o'clock in the afternoon, a new wave of Stukas bombed the whole length of Mareuil. Fortunately, the bombs fell beyond the limits of the village, and they did little damage. Since the Champagne cellars were too far from our neighborhood, we took refuge in our house cellar, the ceiling of which was well vaulted, and our panicked neighbors came to join us. My mother, also rather panicked, presented to everyone a cube of sugar dipped in mint liqueur for comfort! My father hid his head behind a tub, and I kept looking at the vaulted ceiling, hoping that a bomb would not pierce it. My sister Rolande, who had been talking with Monsieur and Madame Defoin, our neighbors from across the street, did not have time to come back to our house. Thus, she went in the Defoins' house. Not seeing her in our cellar and not knowing where the bombs had fallen, we were very afraid that something bad had happened to her. My mother called her in vain. When the planes had gone, Rolande came back home. She told us that, when the bombs were falling, Monsieur Defoin clutched a shaking wardrobe and she clung to his jacket as if that could protect her! From that day, we slept in the cellar, and some soldiers came to sleep in our bedrooms. The following days, bombings and machine-gun fire continued around the region. We had to be very cautious when we wanted to go somewhere.

Then, on May 21, after many others from Mareuil had done so, my family fled to escape the war that was getting closer. In fact, my family was evacuated by Ponts et Chaussées,[3] the governmental agency that employed my father. He did not leave the village until June 10, the date of the official evacuation of the Marne department.

Our exode[4] went fairly well, unlike that of thousands of people who died on the roads. (That was the fate of a neighboring family: the wife of Emile Gilles and her children.) A truck from the Ponts et Chaussées took us from Mareuil to Sézanne and then to Romilly, where we waited for a train for many long hours. We were seven altogether: my mother and her six children. I was the eldest followed by my sisters Jeanne, Rolande, and Micheline. My brother Roger was almost ten, and baby Jean was just nine months old. Roger was completely oblivious to the danger. I still remember that interminable wait on the platform of the railroad station, along with a large crowd of people who, like us, were fleeing the horrors of the war. During the whole afternoon, the only trains that passed by were troop transports. There was an air alert, and I became very anxious. I was asking myself whether we would get to our destination safe and sound. We were going south to Tamnay, the town of my father's family, right in the middle of rural France.

Finally, in the middle of the night, we were able to board a train, which took five hours to get us to Troyes.[5] This train, which came from God knows where, was already full of people evacuating like us. We had a very hard time finding a space to fit us all. We were packed like sardines and could hardly breathe as we were so close to each other. An attack of panic drove all these people toward some more or less precise destination. What was important was to flee the war, the bombs, the armies that were invading the country. And still, at this time, we hoped that the enemy would be stopped. What a delusion!

During the ride between Romilly and Troyes, the train stopped several times. At one of these stops, I remember seeing a man running along the tracks, who yelled incoherent words and especially: "You saw them? They fell from the trains!" Of course, we had seen nothing of the sort. This poor man, like many others at that time of misery, must have lost his mind. During the whole of this incredibly uncomfortable trip, I carried my little brother Jean under my arm. I was concerned about his health because, as he was so tossed around, he had become inert and vomited all the milk we gave him. When we arrived at dawn, we were received by a French Boy Scout unit who gave us a breakfast and who comforted the most tired, the old people, and directed the sick to a place where they could be treated.

Our wait for another train lasted a good part of the day, which seemed to be an eternity. In the afternoon, there was an air alert but no bombing. In the evening, we boarded a train going to Laroche-Migennes. There, we got a connection to Clamecy, where we arrived at sunset. That night, we slept on straw in a room behind the railroad station. Finally, the next day, another train took us to our destination: Tamnay. As noted above, as a state employee, my father had to stay behind in Mareuil but was ordered to leave after the official evacuation of the Marne department was declared on June 10. After five days on the very dangerous roads, he managed to reach Tamnay and our family by bicycle.

Several days after our arrival in Tamnay, I went to Villars, the hamlet where the foster parents of my mother lived. My sisters, brothers, and I always considered them as our maternal grandparents: grandma and grandpa Perceau. I wanted to find work, for we did not know how long our *exode* would last, and my family might not have any income. I sought a job at a pharmacy in Moulins-Engilbert but was not hired. My grandma suggested that I try my luck in nearby Saint-Honoré-les-Bains, a small city famous as a spa. I followed her suggestion. In Saint-Honoré I discovered that the pharmacist, Monsieur Chalon, had been mobilized.

Nevertheless, I was received by Madame Chalon. This lady was not a pharmacist but helped her father-in-law who, although retired, had returned to work under the circumstances. At that point, because of the flow of refugees, the city was overpopulated. That justified the hiring of an assistant pharmacist, especially since Madame Chalon was pregnant. The decision was not made immediately. I gave the telephone number of a café close to Tamnay. Two days later, Madame Chalon asked me to start work on June 1. From that day on, I stayed with the Perceaus in Villars.

On Sunday, June 16, I went to Tamnay on my bicycle, and, halfway there, I met my father, who had arrived the day before. I was overjoyed to see him again, for, without any news of him for about three weeks, we were very worried about him. The next day, June 17, when I arrived at the pharmacy, I saw a crowd in front of the door. In this crowd there were many people who had evacuated like us, including a physician, Doctor Du Pasquier. The Chalon family had hired three maids, including my sister Jeanne. They told me that the whole Chalon family had left. Panic had reached this region. People thought they would find safety in flight. I must say that, in this particular case, with the head of the household off in the military, this frenzy, considering the sheer scale of the debacle of the French armies, was quite excusable.

Over the next two months, I lived an unforgettable experience. At the age of nineteen, as a simple assistant pharmacist, I managed the only open pharmacy in a whole region. I had the satisfaction of having done well and earned the esteem of everyone. At first, confronting the unexpected situation, I was perplexed about what to do, but I nevertheless opened the store. There was a rush of people through the door, and I did not know where to start. Around one o'clock in the afternoon, I was able to go eat lunch in Villars with Jeanne. The other maids went home and were to come back in the evening.

Elie, pharmacist.

One of them, Solange Desgranges, came back around four o'clock and told me that the Germans were arriving. How to describe what I felt at this moment? Like most of the French, I felt that this was the collapse of my country. Everything was crumbling. Some people standing by the door of the pharmacy counseled me to flee. But someone came to tell us that Marshal Pétain[6] had called for an armistice. Hearing that, I decided to stay put. That evening, while alone with Solange, we asked ourselves where we should hide the money that the pharmacy had received that day. After deliberating, I chose an empty box of poison and placed it in the cabinet for dangerous products. After we closed shop, I returned to Villars, and Solange was taken in by a neighbor.

The next day, Tuesday, June 18, I came back to the pharmacy with my sister Jeanne. The other maid, Jacqueline, came back in mid-morning. Still without a boss, we decided to occupy the house so that we could keep it from being looted and to stay on call at night. Electric power had been down but was restored during the day. After we had closed shop, around six thirty, we turned the radio on, and it is thus, by chance, that we heard General de Gaulle reading his famous call to resistance. I only remember hearing him criticize Marshal Pétain for having called for an armistice. From that instant, we began to regain hope. After that, every evening, we listened to Radio London, and had the chance to hear General de Gaulle several times.

In the first days of my activity, the mayor, Monsieur Duriaux, asked a refugee who was a pharmacist to work with me. Seeing how good a job I was doing and that I knew well my profession, the latter assured the mayor that I was very capable of handling things, and he returned to where he was living. During these two months, I prepared a great number of medicines. It happened that I was awakened one night to make some rye ergot pills that I had had no time to prepare during the day. Because of the curfew, I had to make them in the kitchen under the glow of candles. At nineteen, I seemed to be physically younger than I was, and some people wondered if they could entrust their prescriptions to me. The doctors with whom I had a good relationship would reassure them on this score. I often met with Doctors Segard and Sylvestre.

My father returned to Mareuil after the arrival of the Germans. He found our house totally looted. Only the springs were left on our beds. The silver cutlery had disappeared as well as my violin. My mother returned home, with my sisters and brothers, around July 14. Thus, I stayed behind alone with Solange and Jacqueline.

At the beginning of August, the Chalon family began to come back to Saint-Honoré. Monsieur Chalon, Senior, and his wife with their daughter and son-in-law were the first to return. They had become separated from the rest of the family and had taken refuge in La Souterraine. After his return, on some evenings, Monsieur Chalon would join us to listen to de Gaulle on the radio. Having heard that we did that, the mayor gave us a severe reprimand.[7] The younger Madame Chalon, with her one-year old daughter, Françoise, as well as her mother, Madame Feral, and her grand-mother Madame Audoux, had been in Besse-en-Chandesse; they waited for some news from Madame Chalon's husband. Having

Solange, Elie, and Jeanne in Saint-Honoré-les-Bains, 1940.

Jeanne, Elie, and Jacqueline in Saint-Honoré-les-Bains, 1940.

learned that he was a prisoner of war, they returned to Saint-Honoré on August 15. Several days later, Madame Chalon gave birth to another little girl, Anne-Marie. After that time, the members of this family considered me more or less one of them.

I left Saint-Honoré at the end of November 1940. It was in January 1941 that I learned that Monsieur Chalon had returned to his pharmacy, but I met him for the first time only after I returned from Germany in 1945.

CHAPTER 3

Back Home under German Occupation

When I returned home, I tried to find an assistant pharmacist job, but I had no luck. I found a temporary job with the Ponts et Chaussées to remove from the roads the snow that had fallen heavily in December and had been making traffic difficult in the region.

In Mareuil, there was a bookstore managed by Monsieur Fernand Jardret, who represented the Messageries Hachette.[1] He had three employees who made rounds selling newspapers in the region. At the beginning of 1941, one of these employees left him. Because I was a good customer of the bookstore and I liked commerce, Jardret asked me to replace that fellow. He had the most important of the rounds of the towns covered. To convince me to take the job, Jardret promised to leave the management of the bookstore to me because he intended to leave the region for health reasons. I accepted, and it was the first Sunday of January 1941 that I took up the rounds with the former seller, who showed me his route. I had a woman's bicycle, and it was hard to ride in the snow.

The rounds consisted of Tauxières, Louvois, Le Craon de Ludes, Mailly, Verzenay, Verzy, and, at first, Villers-Marmery and

Trépail. To return to Mareuil, we went through Bouzy and Ambonnay. That first day, we did around forty miles on our bicycles, and the next day when I did that route all alone, it was still in the snow. I remember that in the evening of that first solo ride, I had a very hard time climbing the last slope on the bicycle. At the outer edge of Avenay, I ate a little piece of bread left from my lunch to regain some strength. There was a thaw the next day, but in the evening I found myself in a snow storm. The next day, black ice had the best of me as I was leaving Mareuil, and I found myself on the ground. I did not insist on going any further.

I bought a good bicycle with a brake on the hub, and two days later, I was back on the roads. At first, I had only Parisian newspapers as dailies. What helped my sales were periodicals and books. I sold quite a few books costing twenty *sous*.[2] I also had customers for more serious books and illustrated periodicals for the young. In particular, there was *Les belles histoires de vaillance*,[3] a magazine the sale of which the distributing services of Hachette forbade. However, this publication was given to me by the new parish priest of Mareuil, Gabriel Favréaux, and I gladly distributed it. I would sell my papers by shouting, and I had my favorite slogans. For example: "*Paris-Soir*, the newest lies from Berlin!" I still think that I was lucky that that did not get me into trouble. In Verzenay, I had a friend who distributed pictures of General de Gaulle. He would give me some, and, one evening, with my pockets full of these pictures, I passed through a troop of German soldiers on maneuvers under the command of a general.

I had constructed a basket for my bicycle, larger than those usually used for my trade. I had also a sort of box on the rear luggage carrier to hold my lunch bag. There was not much in it. Rarely was there any meat! Generally, there were only rutabagas and a few potatoes. Usually I ate my lunch at a bistro in Mailly when I had finished my rounds in that village. Sometimes I would stop before that time to recuperate because I was so hungry.

Every morning, I would start out with one hundred pounds of papers on my bicycle. After some weeks, the Sunday newspapers were no longer printed. That gave me a day off. Since I did not have many customers in the villages of Villers-Marmery and Trépail, I reduced my itinerary, and ended my rounds in Verzy. To come back,

I would climb the slope of the Faux de Verzy[4] on foot, pushing my bicycle. I still had close to ten miles to go to get home. During the summer vacation, I invited one or another of my friends to follow me on what they thought was a little ride. They returned home dead tired, and none took up again my invitation.

In the last year I held this job, the Reims newspapers looked for sellers. I thus inherited the distribution of the *Eclaireur de l'Est* and of the *Nord Est*, with one requirement: collect subscriptions. That meant that I would need to deliver newspapers to 650 mailboxes every day. Besides riding my bicycle, I often ran several miles on foot. As my customers paid their subscription weekly, I would receive payments on Fridays and Saturdays. Sometimes I would enter the house of some clients at the time of their meals, and, with certain farmers or vineyard owners, I would smell a good aroma from the kitchen. That was hard on me, for I had so little to eat in my lunch bag. Besides black ice, I rode in all kinds of weather, including rain and snow storms. In the winter, I was cold, and some mornings my tears would ice up and stick to my eye lids. In the summer, I was dying under the heat. In the summers of 1941 and 1942, the temperature reached around one hundred degrees Fahrenheit. I had a large number of customers, and I was earning a decent salary, but it was hard work.

At the beginning of 1942, the Messageries gave us some anti-Semite pamphlets to distribute. The cover of these things had a big yellow Star of David like the one Jews were to sew on their clothes. I was revolted by these pamphlets. However, fearing an inspection by an agent of the Messageries, I put a few of these required pamphlets in my basket, but I never delivered any. My colleagues also refused to deliver them. One Sunday, as most Sundays, I went with some friends to the movies in Epernay. Out of bravado, I pinned one of these covers on my coat. I walked from Mareuil and back, going through Aÿ, with that star on me. I did not do it again because I learned later that young people who had done the same were arrested by the police and their identity cards were stamped "affiliated with Jews."

⚔ Obviously, I did this job under the German occupation. And, under this occupation, life in the Champagne region was very hard.

We went through a dark period indeed. We suffered all sorts of privations, especially hunger, which was the worst. Nevertheless, my friends and I tried to overcome these hardships by maintaining our cultural activities. As I previously mentioned, in Epernay, I played in a jazz orchestra directed by Roger Thomas, an excellent trumpet player. Furthermore, in Mareuil, the little group of JOC took up its activity again with the new parish priest, Gabriel Favréaux. He had been a troop chaplain and was appointed by the Diocese of Reims to the parish church of Mareuil at the beginning of the occupation.[5] Since the meetings of the group often lasted beyond the time of the curfew, we had to be careful to avoid German patrols on our way home.

At the beginning of 1941, the church choir was reconstituted. It was composed of ten teenagers, most of them musicians, and I took up again its direction. Father Favréaux, who was an organist, gave us advice. At the time of certain holy days, older people would join us. At that time, we sang the mass in Latin, and we had learned different musical masses, hymns, and motets in polyphony. All that demanded a commitment and forced us to do more than our best, to keep our heads high despite the humiliating defeat of our country, the vexations of the collaborators, and the difficulty of finding food.

CHAPTER 4

In Bondage
Forced Labor in the Todt Organization

In 1942, the Allies began to carry out large bombing raids over Germany and Italy. Some evenings, we would hear the noise of hundreds of planes flying over Mareuil. This was comforting in a way because it gave me and many others the certitude of our liberation. Still, however, this fearsome rumbling was rather frightening.

That same year, as an answer to the Nazis' demands for French manpower to work in Germany, the Vichy government created what it called *La Relève*,[1] that is, the voluntary departure of French workers in exchange, supposedly, for the repatriation of an equal number of compatriot prisoners of war. This maneuver was nothing more than a fraud and was in fact a failure. I recall that, from that point forward, those who kept a picture of Marshal Pétain in their homes ended up feeding it to the fire in their kitchen stove.

After the failure of several attempts to obtain the number of workers required, the Germans put pressure on the Vichy government that was collaborating with them so that it would take more effective measures. It is then that the law of September 4, 1942, was passed. This law stated that any eighteen- to fifty-year-old man and any twenty-one- to thirty-five-year-old woman could be drafted to do any work that the government judged to be in the interest of the nation. This was a requisition and deportation for work in Germany—pure and simple. This law was a precursor of another that established the Service du Travail Obligatoire (STO), the Required Work Service.

Starting in October, I saw people leave in groups of different sizes after several calls. It was a dramatic time. All those who were forced to go work in the country of the enemy knew what was waiting for them: hunger (which most had experienced already in the preceding two years), mistreatment, and bombings. There was a distressing question: How many would never come back? It was impossible to escape this deportation where I lived. There was no place to hide, and denunciation was always to be feared. I remember that one day someone told me: "It will be good for them, the young, to go to Germany. That will tame them!" Certainly, such people could not be counted on to help me escape. The Résistance was not really organized for that, especially in my region, until the end of 1943.

Elie in 1942.

➤ Because I was an independent worker, I was not registered on one of these lists that businesses were required, under the Required Work Service law, to keep at the disposal of the German Work Service authorities. Nevertheless, on the evening of February 1, 1943, as I returned from my press route, my mother announced to me that I had received my requisition order for the Todt Organization[2] in Soissons.

This was one of the sites where, generally, the young men of my generation were sent to work on the construction projects of the Todt Organization in France. Major construction sites included those of the Atlantic wall and the submarine bases of Lorient, Saint Nazaire, and La Rochelle. In the region of Soissons, the Todt Organization was building a whole series of bunkers. The most important construction site was located in Margival.

I decided not to respond to this first call. Fernand Jadret, the Mareuil bookstore manager for whom I was a seller, attempted to intervene at the *sous-préfecture*[3] of Epernay but without success. Two weeks later, a second requisition order had arrived at my home. At that moment, the question for me became: Should I obey the order or risk being sent to work in Germany? After much reflection with my family, I decided to go to Soissons, approximately fifty miles from Mareuil. It was really impossible for me to do otherwise. As soon as I had received my requisition order, my food ration tickets were stopped. I did not know where I could hide, and, in the final analysis, my fate looked much better than that of my friends, who all had been sent to Germany. I must say that, at the beginning of 1943, the word *maquis* did not mean anything more than the shrub that grows in Corsica![4] And I must add that the intention of all those who were deported was to work as little as possible and to engage in sabotage every time there was an opportunity.

Thus, one afternoon, I presented myself to the German Work Service agency in Reims. There, I met a fellow who was in the same situation as I was. His name was Edmond Vermand, and he came from Pontfaverger. Since there was no train for Soissons that evening, we spent the night in a lodging center in the railroad station yard.

The next morning, we presented ourselves at the headquarters of the Todt Organization (*Frontführung*) at Soissons. There was a strange atmosphere in that city. In the streets, many people were moving around like automatons, with clothes more or less ragged, dirty, shod with wooden soled shoes, their haversack on one shoulder. On the whole, all these people looked prostrate with grief. They soon would be my workmates.

Once Edmond and I registered, we were locked up for three days in a closed down movie theater with other requisitioned men already there waiting to be directed to one of the camps of the region and to be assigned to a construction firm. Three days without going outside seemed like an eternity! Thoughts of escape came to my mind. But to go where? It was a cruel dilemma. Moreover, I could not forget what might happen to members of my family if I escaped.

Our waiting ended on the fourth day when the chief of the German firm Förster came to get us. He took us to a camp located on a plateau at the limits of the village of Neuville-sur-Margival. Thus, I found myself in a room inside a wooden barrack. In it, there were bunk beds. My roommates were all Arabs. I chose a top bunk. Across my barrack there was a small prisoner-of-war camp, which was full of Africans and Muslims. I could see them, some evenings, do their prayers. My camp, which was crossed by a small road, was composed of several barracks, all in wood, one of which was larger than the others. That barrack served as a kitchen and a mess hall. The mess hall, in fact, was used as a sort of theater. The Alix Combelle orchestra played there. Cadyn, known in France as *le roi de la pince*,[5] who would rip in two a deck of cards with his hands, gave a show, as did others. The entrances of the camp were indicated by large placards on which were painted the German eagle and the swastika. That gave us the idea to baptize the camp as "the hotel of the black crow."

Every morning at breakfast we were given a liquid concoction of roasted barley, which passed for coffee. Considering the privations we were suffering since 1940, it was nevertheless tolerable. I must note that we took advantage of the chaos that existed in the system, and we did our best to get a few days off every two weeks. This gave us the opportunity to bring back to the camp some food that permitted us to endure. Of course, these fraudulent leaves were not without risk. Some men were brought back to camp by the police or the Gestapo. And the men of the French Milice,[6] who were the guards of the Soissons' *caserne*, took pleasure in beating up those who were arrested as they returned from a false leave.

One morning, at the time of our "sock juice" (the aforementioned "coffee"), one of these men from the Milice came to pay us a visit. He started by giving a propaganda speech about the "National Revolution" of Pétain and continued with anti-Semitic remarks. I remember that, as more and more of us came in with our "coffee cups," we surrounded him in a circle that became more and more compact without saying a word. Our silence probably seemed threatening to him. Did he become afraid? Did an "accident" happen to him? He never came back. We never saw him again.

As far as work was concerned, I was "hired" by the German firm Förster, which was in charge of the construction of a concrete road between the railroad station of Vauxhaillon and an immense bunker in the valley of Margival. I learned much later that this bunker was to be Hitler's headquarters in case of an allied invasion on the shores of France. He came to it only once. Another German firm by the name of Keufer was building fortified works. This led us to make a pun with the names of those two firms.[7]

Among those who ordered us around were two Germans from the Todt Organization and a Polish civilian, who served as interpreter. Since we had a tough time remembering their names, we gave them nicknames. The chief of the construction site was baptized the "Négus," the other, who had a large mustache, "Vercingétorix," and the Polish guy "Staviski."[8] While we made fun of them, these three were really hard on us.

As far as I was concerned, one or the other would harass me about this or that, and I was always given work beyond my strength. As I complained about that to my workmates, one of them told me: "Of course, you always seem to laugh at them!" To that, I replied: "Surely not; I cannot help it, it's my natural expression." It is true that, when I was young, my face always shone with a sort of a mocking smile.

The Todt Organization had a cosmopolitan population. It included German public work firms, as well as equivalent French firms, specializing in concrete constructions, bunkers, roads, railroads, and so on. In my area, the Drouard enterprise from the Paris region was involved in the construction of bunkers. I believe that, for this enterprise, the Todt Organization was one of its clients like any other and that the workers on the site were its employees. As far as the requisitioned workers like me were concerned, they were from all kinds of professional walks of life. I still thought of myself as an assistant pharmacist, and I worked alongside barbers, bank employees, butchers, a variety of merchants, and also people from the construction industry. The spectacle of the activity on a Todt construction site gave a strange impression. It was as if one looked at a slow motion movie. All the workers applied themselves to move with a well-calculated slowness. If one of us made a seemingly fast movement, he would be hailed by a: "Do you work for the victory?"

My first work day was incredibly hard. I had to use a shovel to load a concrete mixer with gravel and sand, and to unload ballast with a special fork. I was not used to this kind of work, and my limbs felt as if they had been crushed. Moreover, there were these Germans who did not understand why I was so slow at my work. Indeed, I simply could not keep up with a normal rhythm. There was also, as in the case of all my wretched workmates, a will to slow down to a maximum the completion of Nazi projects. It was extremely painful for me to get up in the mornings. I was aching all over, and my joints literally felt as if they were rusty. With time, my body got used to this life, but not my spirit.

Our slowing down of the work sometimes took on a comical tinge. Here are some examples. Two men would carry a framing plank when one worker could have carried four without much effort; when an overseer was not around while we were spraying concrete, we would sink into it rail sections that were servicing the construction site. One day, when I was pumping water in a Regulus concrete mixer, which ran continuously, I did it so slowly that the concrete came out half dry. No need to describe the reaction of the overseer who was at the point where the concrete came out! Another time, at noon, when the soup had not yet arrived, the overseers ordered us to continue to work until it was delivered. A moment later, right after some concrete had come out of a mixer, some joker yelled: "To the soup!" Right then, all, as one man, left the construction site and rushed to the mess hall. But there was still no soup. Fortunately, it came a few minutes later, but in the meantime several cubic feet of concrete had dried and were no longer any good. It is then that I first heard the word "sabotage" yelled out in German!

Very often, our acts of sabotage were for us a source of internal rejoicing. For example, when we drowned rails in the concrete, they obviously were missing in the inventory. Then, our overseer would take a few men to another construction site to bring some back, believing that they had been swiped, and that would lead to some great rows between overseers, which gave us a concealed deep jubilation under a contrite air. We were oblivious to the consequences that these little actions could have had. When it came to repression, the Nazis were without pity.

Despite all our efforts to block the machinery, we were at times forced to accelerate the rhythm of our work. Thus, one evening, a half-hour before the end of my shift, I found myself left alone to feed with gravel a Regulus mixer that had an endless screw. The job consisted of filling the bucket of the mixer fast enough so that the screw was never visible. After a few moments, it was no longer drops of sweat that ran down my nose, but a veritable stream. I also remember that I almost collapsed the first time someone put a bag of cement on my shoulders. One hundred pounds! I had never carried a load so heavy. It was agony when full railroad cars had to be unloaded, and the bags had to be carried several yards away.

The teams that worked on the construction of bunkers had a very difficult schedule. When it was time to pour the concrete for one of these buildings, the workers had shifts of twenty-four to forty-eight hours without a break. Soup and cognac were brought to them on the construction site. Some evenings, overseers would pass through the barracks asking for volunteers, but they had no success. We refused to help our conquerors.

The three months that I spent in the Soissons region were very hard on me, but I felt lucky not to be in Germany. And, like my friends, I thought that the landing of the Allies on our shores would soon take place. It was during this period, however, that I discovered life in common with others and worked in a team, engaged in very hard work, above my physical capacities, while exposed to all kind of weather. But I also lived a tremendous experience of fraternity and solidarity.

As a Christian and a member of the JOC, I believed firmly that I could in such circumstances be a witness for my faith without proselytizing to my wretched comrades. I thought that it would not always be easy, for we were living some exceptional moments, and, despite our obliviousness, we were in fact meant for more dramatic hours. The rest of my story will demonstrate how true that was.

CHAPTER 5

Deported to Germany

On February 16, 1943, the French government enacted a new law instituting the Service du Travail Obligatoire (STO), that is "Required Work Service," for the classes of the years 1940, 1941, and 1942.[1] Being of the 1941 class, I found myself under this sort of disguised mobilization. And naturally, following this situation, what was bound to happen, happened. One morning at the beginning of June, when I arrived at the construction site, my workmates and I were handed a piece of paper that notified us of our imminent departure for Germany. We were told that we would leave from the Soissons *caserne* on June 9, in the afternoon. We were not told where exactly we would go. However, we knew that a few days earlier the British Royal Air Force had destroyed two dams in the Ruhr region. We all were convinced right away that this would be our first destination.

On the evening of June 8, after receiving this order, we left the construction site so we could go home to see our families and collect some supplies. Thus, I returned to Mareuil for a night and a half day. I went around the village to say goodbye to several people, including Father Favréaux, who gave me his benediction. Nobody suggested the possibility of escape from the order I had received, which I considered, as did my comrades, a deportation.² This happened despite the efforts of Monsieur Pierre Tantet,³ a village notable who lived close to my home. Unbeknown to me, this man was, in fact, at the time, organizing a resistance network which he called by its initials CDLR. These initials stood for Ceux de la Résistance, "Those of the Resistance." At that moment, Monsieur Tantet did not have the means to offer me a way to escape my deportation. I had no other option but to obey my order. And then, I thought about the fate of the village's prisoners of war and its two dozen young men already in Germany. I felt guilty in a way for not sharing that fate. Moreover, I had to think about the eventual but real reprisals that might befall my family if I escaped. Furthermore, there was the risk of denunciation.

Obviously, in the Champagne country, my farewells to friends were well washed down, and I ended up quite plastered! That helped me forget for a moment the anxiety and fear of the future that I felt. On my last day in Mareuil, after the noon meal, my father accompanied me to the railroad station of Avenay, where I was to take a train for Reims, and then to Soissons. When we parted, I saw big tears rolling down his cheeks. I waited until the train left to let mine flow freely. It has always been with great emotion when I have relived this moment in my mind. The question was: "Will we see each other again?" Who could answer? There was no real reason to be optimistic. Like all my comrades, I dreaded the sort of treatment that the Nazis could inflict on us when they had us in their claws. And, as we left for Germany, we knew that we would be subjected to the bombings of the Allied forces. We too would be among their targets.

— On June 9, in the afternoon, about one thousand of us were in the yard of the Soissons *caserne*. When the signal for departure was given, Germans and Czechs in Todt uniforms armed with submachine guns escorted us as we marched toward the railroad station through the outer boulevards. For several months, the Germans had gotten used to boisterous demonstrations, which accompanied every departure of requisitioned workers for Germany. That day was no exception. All of us made quite a rumpus all along the way to the station. We sang the "Internationale" and the "Marseillaise," and slogans were uttered loudly: "Down with Pétain!" "Laval to the firing squad!"[4] I believe that we even yelled "Death to Hitler!" Moreover, a large crowd followed us and urged us on.

As we arrived at the station, we saw that the locomotive of our train was decked out with tricolor flags and the rail cars were covered with all sorts of graffiti: the letter V, Crosses of Lorraine, which was the symbol of de Gaulle, hammers and sickles, and anti-German and anti-Vichy slogans. Our guards thrashed about like devils to make us erase the graffiti. However, as we were erasing in one place, new graffiti would appear elsewhere. This lasted for quite a while before the train moved off.

All of us attempted to persuade each other that we would be back home in six months. We were fooling ourselves.

As other young Christians, militants from the JOC or from several other Catholic action movements, who were leaving to be subjected to an ordeal that we all dreaded, I felt called to be a witness of my faith to my comrades. As I said earlier, I believed that it would be difficult. I would have to partake in the hardest jobs and perhaps receive only meager nutrition. I would have to sustain the morale of those who might break down, and I would have to participate in actions that could harm the Nazi system. That meant that I would have to refuse anything that could be a cushy job. This is why I never mentioned that I was an assistant pharmacist, not wanting to be given the job of a nurse or something of that nature. In other words, I wanted to work. Despite the fear of the sacrifices that I would endure, I confided in God, praying that He would spare me from great suffering. How many times have I repeated Jesus' words on the eve of His passion: "Father, if You want, take away from me this cup, but Your will be done."

—⚓— The train was made up of cars without corridors and, of course, without toilets. Thus, it was in the least comfort that we were leaving. The train left the Soissons station at the end of the afternoon and the first stop was Compiègne. From there, it went north passing through Hirson.

Our first night was spent in the marshaling yards of Aulnoye, our last stop before the Belgian frontier. All along the journey, our guards were on the running boards of the cars, their pistols in hand. Whenever we looked out of a window or passed a French flag out, they would shoot at us.

The crossing of Belgium took most of the next day. After going through Mons, the train stopped in Braine-Lecomte. I will never forget the atmosphere that reigned in that station. The train was stopped on a siding, but the passengers in the station, who were numerous that morning, came to see us. They clung to our cars; they embraced us; they sang the "Marseillaise." It was an indescribable rumpus. The Germans tried to keep them from the cars in vain! We shed tears with the Belgians, who already knew what the deportation of their youth was like. When the train left, it went in the direction of Brussels and made a stop in the Laaken station. There, we were given permission to go to the latrines. But for me and for many others, it was for naught. The nervous tension and anxiety had made us constipated! After that stop, the train went toward Holland. In the evening, it arrived at the little border station of Dalheimd. There, the stop was rather long. Anguish began to get a hold of us: we were about to enter that *Reich* that wanted to make slaves out of us. The train started to move at the end of the evening. Now we were in this fearsome Germany. We had always believed that nothing worse could have happened to us. As far as I was concerned, I had the impression that a door had slammed shut behind me. It was as if I were entering a different world from the one in which I had lived until then.

At dusk, there was a halt in a small station. Our guards made us come down from the train and took us to an SS *caserne*, where we were served a cup of soup in a large room fitted out with a lot of marble. The atmosphere was as icy as the attitude of the SS who shoved us to move faster. People from the village had gathered at the railroad crossing where the train was stopped. They were curious. Some among us could not help themselves from addressing some coarse words to the young girls present. That was answered by invectives from those who had heard them and understood. It was night when the train left. I fell asleep and woke up only when the train arrived at the Hagen station because of the yelling of our escort.

When all of us were assembled on the station's platform, standing on top of a wooden box, the *Lagerführer*, or head of the camp, a man named Wolf, "favored" us with a long harangue. He warned us that any pro-communist demonstration would be severely punished, as would any other action that undermined discipline. We were now in the German *Reich* and we had to obey! After this "reassuring" speech, we were regrouped in a yard at the end of the freight station. We spent the day there, not knowing what our final destination would be. I thought, with good reason, that it would be one of the dams that the British had destroyed recently, but this still was not certain. During this day spent in that station, my comrades and I had the occasion to see for the first time Soviet prisoners of war. A big "SU" was painted on the back of their jackets. Their appearance was so bad that some of my comrades expressed their dismay. They said: "It's not possible that these are the pals of Stalin!"

During the afternoon, children came to see us and played with us. From time to time on the high road that looked down on the yard, we could see very young boys of the *Hitlerjugend*, the Hitler Youth, in uniform with helmets on their heads and daggers in their belts. For all of us, that was quite a surprise. And then, a dramatic event took place that added to our helplessness, and we were all deeply distressed over it. One of the boys who had come to see us fell asleep on the ledge of the retaining wall of the road. That wall was approximately fourteen feet high. All of a sudden, the child fell. We picked him up dead. Despite the hate we had at that time about everything German, that was quite a shock to us and we were heartbroken.

—⊁— With whom would I share this disguised captivity? Most of them had been with me in the camp of Neuville-sur-Margival. There was François Corbeil of Houilles, whose father was English and a clerk; René Détante of Mantes-Gassicourt, who was a mechanic; the shopkeeper Gilbert Delahaye, nicknamed Gigi; the tall Pavin, who argued loudly that we had left France for only six months; and three others from Bruyères-et-Montbérault, a village near Laon. There was also the Serb Krujac, a farm worker who was requisitioned before he could return home; Camille Balloche of Houdan; and the fat

Domisse, who was a horticulturist in La Ferté-sous-Jouarre. These, I can say, were my very first buddies. I would get to know others as I went from one camp to another.

Around seven in the evening, we were packed into freight cars, designed to transport either eight horses or forty men. Our train went through the region that had been ravaged by the waters of the bombed-out Möhnetal Dam. Along the railroad line, we could see the old tracks swept into the fields, full of sludge. The dam was our destination. We arrived in the middle of the night in the freight station of Neheim-Hüsten. As we got out of the cars, there was a great scramble because the train barely stopped, giving us hardly the time to get to our suitcases. We were taken to the passenger station where everyone tried to rest as best as he could. But, since there was not enough space for everybody, I decided to spend the night outside on the grass. And, to crown it all, a nearby city—probably Hagen—sustained a bombing that lasted nearly an hour. From where we were, we could see the glow of the fires. That certainly reassured us as to what would happen later!

The next morning, we were transported in trucks of the NSKK, the National Sozialistische Kraftwagen Korps, or National Socialist Truck Corps, to the dam on the Möhne River. There, we were divided into two groups in two buildings of the little village of Delecke-über-Soest. One group was put in a gymnasium. The other, which included me, was sent to a beach building, the walls of which were like an openwork fence made up of logs. At first, we slept on straw spread on the floor. Later, we were given bunk beds.

Even the most traumatic events have, as everybody knows, their somewhat comical side. Our experience was no exception. I remember a fellow, more or less innocent, who kept repeating that he had nothing to do there because he had been requisitioned for Soissons. I still can see him sitting on his suitcase. Finally, he went down the road all the way to the Neheim station. There, the police arrested him and brought him back to our camp *manu militari*.

At the time of our arrival at the Möhnetal Dam, following the flood provoked by its breach, there was, in the prisoners of war and requisitioned Russians camps, a typhus epidemic that devastated an important part of that population. Fortunately, we escaped that epidemic. At the beginning of our forced stay, we were given soup twice per day. But that did not last long. At noon, we were given the first in a mess hall that was close to the reconstruction site of the dam. However, this soup was more often than not water with red cabbage and turnips that were as hard as wood and inedible. In the evening, the meal was not much more substantial. With the soup, we received a ration of three hundred grams of black bread for twenty-four hours, along with twenty grams of margarine and a slice of salami or some artificial honey or some treacle. Needless to say, with this diet, our health quickly suffered. We became very thin and weak. We already had suffered from hunger since the beginning of the war, but we were about to know worse.

CHAPTER 6

Work at the Möhnetal Dam

In addition to suffering pangs of hunger, I found the working conditions at the Möhnetal Dam extremely hard. As I said before, among my workmates there were young men from all kinds of professions: bureaucrats, barbers, shopkeepers, students, and at least a few workers and artisans from the building trade. I also got to know Torremans, a Belgian miner whom we nicknamed "Charleroi."[1] At first, our work consisted of clearing away from the dam the rubble left by the bombing. We had to carry loads beyond our strength. For example, we had to move electric wire poles on a ground full of rocks gullied by the water that had escaped through the breach of the dam. We also had to clear away the debris after explosive charges had been set off on the flanks of the breach. This was to eliminate cracks produced by the explosion of the initial bombing. As we worked at the height of thirty to fifty meters, I had to control the vertigo I experienced. From the base of the dam, we had to climb back up by pulling ourselves with ropes. After some weeks of that, our clothes had become like rags, and we looked like tramps.

Our work schedule was the following: one week, from seven in the morning to seven in the evening, and the next week, from seven in the evening to seven in the morning. At first, during the night shift, the site was illuminated by big carbide lights that left some areas in shadows. The shadows provided a brief respite from time to time. To hide in peace, we devised a trick. On the dam's breach there were sixteen pneumatic hammer drills weighing ninety pounds that got their power from huge compressed air tanks. When no overseer was in sight, we would block the trigger with a rag and wedged the drill between rocks. That made a terrific noise and gave the impression that we were really working hard.

At that time, the scaffold was under construction. A large amount of dirt had been dropped along the wall of the dam on the lake side to form an embankment where the scaffold could be anchored. That scaffold was built by Dutch carpenters and was made entirely of wood. It was twenty meters high (the height of the breach) and approximately two hundred meters long, the distance between the two towers. It had six levels with narrow gauge tracks to deliver materials to the masons. If my memory serves me right, there must have been eight perpendicular platforms served by turntables that all of us called *sauterelles*, "grasshoppers." Ultimately, the lighting of the whole work site was modernized with the installation of more powerful lights suspended from the wall of the dam. During all this preparatory work, teams of specialists probed the dam below the breach to see whether there might be cracks and, of course, to eliminate them.

When everything was ready for reconstruction, hundreds of Italians arrived on the site, most of them masons. Because Italy had been an ally of Nazi Germany, these men had come voluntarily to work in Germany several years earlier. Later, other Italians showed up. These, however, were prisoners of war from the Badoglio army.[2] Painted on the back of their coats were the initials IMI, for Italienische Militär Interniert, or Italian Military Inmates. These poor fellows were in an indescribable state of distress. Their camp, next to mine, was surrounded by barbed wire. I remember that some of them would trade their wedding rings, their watches, and other objects of value for a piece of bread. I was disgusted by the sight of such human deterioration. However, my workmates and I were about to know the same fate.

As the reconstruction began, my team was assigned to haul materials for the masons. Small rail cars full of stones (sandstone from Austria) or mortar came to us by a lift. Then we pushed them to a service platform and operated the *sauterelles* to supply several different points according to need. We had a trick to slow down the work: we would turn the *sauterelles* halfway, and we would push the car on the planks. It would always take some time to get it back on the rails. It would also happen that the cable of the lift would break, sometimes tearing up the locking rails as it went down. That gave us a half-day of rest, unless we were given another chore. At any rate, this was lost time. We would push alternatively cars full of stones and cars full of mortar. Our fingers were coated with mortar that ate our skin. As we unloaded the stones by hand, their scraping would also create open wounds. That made "beautiful" circles of blood near our nails. To minimize the damage to our fingers, we would wrap our hands in pieces of cloth, but it was nevertheless painful. Once, I dropped a stone on one of my fingers. The nail came off a few days later.

Some of my workmates had even harder jobs. They worked at unloading cement and stones under the eye of one overseer for every six men. They were subjected to a hellish rhythm. They were completely depressed. Among them was my Serbian friend Krujac, a fellow who was as hard as a rock. One evening in October, at the end of his shift after dark, he waited for one of his most brutal overseers and gave him a good beating. That surprised overseer never found out who the culprit was.

Once, during the midnight break, two of my workmates and I fell asleep, and we didn't wake up until two in the morning. To get back to the scaffold, we had to pass in front of the barrack of the director of the reconstruction. We passed under the window doubled up so as not to be seen. However, an engineer who was there heard us. He came out with his revolver in his hand. My two co-workers managed to get back up, but I fell. I tried to hide in the shadows, but the engineer saw me and pointed his gun at me. He signaled that I should come to him. Scolding me, he threatened me with a denial of the next soup. But that did not happen.

Night was propitious to absenteeism. Because of that, we devised a plan by which each in turn would go to bed at the midnight break. At the end of the night shift, a fellow worker would hold his hand to present the clocking card and receive the soup tickets of the one who was absent. This ploy was eventually discovered by our overseers and a tighter control forced us to stop our trick.

Until the end of June, the noon soup was served to us temporarily from a field kitchen of a *Gasthof*, a kind of German restaurant, located on the shore of the lake. One day, when our soup was to be served from our camp's kitchen instead, because of some sort of snafu we did not get any soup from either place. Obviously, we were not pleased. We consulted each other to figure out what attitude we should take. We decided to stop working, not knowing what risks we were taking. We would tell each other: "They will not send us to Germany, we are already there! And what was the worst thing that could happen to us? A concentration camp? The difference would be that our camp would be surrounded by barbed wire. What do we care? We are already prisoners!" In fact, we were unaware of the horrors of concentration camps. At any rate, we left for the countryside nearby. Fortunately, no sanction was levied against this sort of strike. We were lucky, for it must be remembered that the Todt Organization reported to the Nazi party and directly to the SS.

The managers of this organization frequently tried to enroll us in enterprises that would compromise our principles. In France, the Todt Organization had recruited musicians to form a band. Although I was a musician, I chose to share the harsh life of Nazi construction sites rather than to wear the uniform of the Todt Organization. In Germany, we were offered the chance to take driving lessons so we could become truck drivers for the NSKK, another organization reporting to the SS. These drivers wore a black uniform. These attempts to lure us into a better position were in vain: none of us fell into the trap. We were once given a physical by some SS. There was no follow-up to it. Our overseers were all members of the Todt Organization, or, in other words, were members of the Nazi party. They included many discharged SS as well as civil engineers of the firm in charge of the reconstruction of the dam. Of course, we quickly gave nicknames to many of them: "green hat," "the wild one," and so forth. One day, for no apparent reason, an old guy told us: "Léon Blum, prima!"[3] This old guy was obviously a socialist and not a Nazi. On the other hand, a fat engineer would call us all Gaullists. We did not deny this epithet! For Nazi propaganda, we were filmed several times. I wonder what is left of these films in the German archives.

At the end of September 1943, the wall of the dam was rebuilt, but there was still much to be done: roads, sluice gates, electric plant, and so on. At that point, we were assigned to another construction site at the foot of the dam. There a concrete platform had to be built. First, we had to clear up the area, and that required putting our hands into putrid stuff. I remember picking up a dead eel in the water that had been stagnant for months. While we were doing this work, we had to avoid touching anything metallic because of frequent electric discharges. One night, we had to rescue a man who got stuck in the anti-mine net that was in the rocks of the site. When this clean-up job was done, carpenters built casting forms ten meters deep and of a width that I have forgotten. These forms had iron bars to reinforce the concrete. When the pouring of the concrete started, we were given the job of vibrating it. For that, we were given some high boots, and we packed the concrete down by walking in it. To keep our balance we held onto the iron bars fixed to the framework with bolts. Engaging in this work all night long was exhausting, and time seemed to pass awfully slowly. Once, as we were working as slowly as possible, our overseer, the one we called "the wild one," stepped into the concrete to show us how to work. But, as the iron bars were not yet secured, he fell into the concrete up to his belly. Then he left us in peace for the rest of the night. On one of the following nights, I was the victim. The concrete came down through a chute of large diameter. As the piping of the chute was more or less tight, it leaked. During a pouring, a pebble hit me in the forehead. I bled profusely, so much so that one of the overseers began to panic. He put a bandage around my head, and I continued to work. Later, my friends told me that I should have pretended to faint, which would have allowed me to go to bed. I must admit that the idea never occurred to me. And then, if I had played that comedy, the same pals of mine would have had to carry me up the framework of the platform, and that would not have been easy.

At the end of October, a diphtheria epidemic severely attacked our ranks. My bunkmate, René Détante, caught it and was hospitalized. Since it was starting to get cold, I borrowed his blankets. The result of my imprudence did not take long to occur. I contracted the illness in turn. One morning, I woke up with a very sore throat and a very high fever. With difficulty I went to the *revier*, that is, the infirmary of the construction site, where a doctor examined the sick. As soon as he looked in my throat, he diagnosed diphtheria. He sent me back to my camp where an ambulance took me to the hospital of Soest, a little town nearby. I found myself in isolation in a room with ten other men, all with diphtheria. This was the first time I was in a hospital, and it is there that I had my first shot. I must say that, since I was half conscious, I did not have any fear.

In that hospital, it must be said that we were very well treated. As for me, it took a good week to get back on my feet. The German nurses, known as *Schwester* (sister), took great care of me and the other men. I still remember the names of two of them: Elfriede and Mathilde, who was the night nurse. The head nurse must have been a convinced Nazi. I remember that she never failed to listen to Hitler every time he was on the radio. The doctor was a very beautiful young woman who spoke excellent French. During one of her visits, she told me: "You are better here than with the Todt Organization, no?" As I acquiesced, she added: "We will try to keep you here as long as possible." Another day, she asked the question: "Aren't you Jewish?" I told her that I was not. Then, she added: "Well, you have a Biblical name — Elie — and you have black and shining eyes." Then, she said: "I'm just joking!"[4] In fact, I believe that indeed she kept us as long as possible, for I stayed a month in the hospital. Looking at my thinness and the degree of my weakness, she had me go through a series of ultraviolet ray treatments. However, what really made me appreciate my stay in the hospital was the food. While not copious, it was much better than that of the camp, and I ate twice a day.

As I had studied the German language for two years and a half before the war, I had put in my luggage a book about German grammar when I left France. As I felt better during my hospital stay, I took out the book and reviewed irregular verbs and vocabulary. That made it possible for me to have conversations with the nurses and improve my knowledge of the language. I made even more progress later on, as I will show in the rest of my story. That turned out to be very useful for me as well as for my camp- and workmates. One of the inconveniences of our situation was that we were locked up during air raid alerts. Some nights, we did not feel very safe as hundreds of planes passed over us. And when they did not drop bombs, the shots from the flak, or anti-aircaft, guns were just as terrifying.

Among us was a Dutch fellow who was so tall that he did not really fit in his bed. Since his four limbs were always bent, we gave him the nickname of *vier Stück*, "Four Pieces." One day, a German journalist, who was rather old, was hospitalized with us. His wife was also hospitalized with scarlet fever in another hospital where she died. When he heard the news, the journalist could not stop crying. He was so inconsolable that he was moved to another room after a man, probably a member of the party, had come to reprimand him. Despite the hate we had for anything German, personally I felt some pity for that journalist. This was even more so since he confided in me because I understood German. I tried to comfort him by evoking the hope of a better world where we would find again those that we had loved in this world. However, I had the impression that I was not getting through to him.

All my comrades, who had passed through this hospital for the same illness as me, were given a leave for the time of their convalescence. Once gone, they never came back. Therefore these leaves were cancelled—just at the time that I got out of the hospital. I thus went back to my camp. It was now a new camp. During my absence, new barracks had been built closer to the dam. It was there that I found again my roommates and where I spent my fifteen days of convalescence before returning to work. During that time, I would get visits from camp policemen. The magic word to get rid of them was "diphtheria." When they heard it, they left in a jiffy.

⟶ The day came—or rather the night—when I had to return to work. It was mid-December. I was assigned to a team whose job was to build a protective embankment of dirt against the wall of the dam. We worked in temperatures of ten degrees Fahrenheit or lower. We had to dig frozen dirt as hard as rock, and, when it was snowing, the dirt stuck to our shovels. We had to load small rail cars that could hold one and a half cubic meter of that dirt. Our overseers wanted us to fill each of these cars in a half-hour. However, we decided to do it in an hour and a half, and we kept that tempo. This work was very hard on us. When we were shoveling, we would sweat. When we stopped between two bunches of cars, we would get cold. Our clogs would stick to the dirt and that made any movement very painful. My ankles became covered with blisters, and that was a real torture.

The first night, as usual, we had a break at midnight. We went to the site's barrack to get soup. However, our overseer announced that there was no soup. On the spot, we decided to leave the work site. In the face of our determination, the overseer told us that he was going to call the *Frontführung* (the main office of the work site), and he threatened us with the worst sanctions. He went back to his office and, as I understood it, he transmitted our decision to stop work and asked for soup to be served to the night shifts. When he came out again, he told us: "Morgen Suppe," "Tomorrow, there will be soup." We then went back to work, and the promise was kept.

The following week, we had a day shift. The weather was better, but my feet hurt just as much. One day, we got one of these small rail cars off the tracks at the time of the noon break. When we returned to work, we had to put it back on the tracks. But since it was below the tracks, we had to push it back up. In principle this was not too difficult to do, but following our determination to resist, we decided to take as much time as possible. Six of us, each armed with a lever, didn't make the car move as much as a hair. Our overseer was yelling at us, but that did not faze us. All of a sudden, full of anger, he put his hands on the car and began to pull it. Then, as one man, we pushed with our levers. In three seconds, the object of our "efforts" was back on the tracks. Sarcastically, we exclaimed: "Sechs Franzosen können nichts; ein Deutscher, alles gut!" "Six Frenchmen can't do anything; one German and all is well!"

That week went by with its share of physical pains: tremendous fatigue, cold, hunger that gnawed at our stomachs. It had been six months since we had left France—our deportation. Our country seemed so far away! We had the impression that we had been in Germany for years. To see peace again and to have a normal life seemed out of reach. Fortunately, we had the will not to let us break down, and, our youth helping, we overcame our moments of despair. And then the Allies were in Italy. We hoped that they would soon be able to invade the whole of Europe. Unfortunately, it took much longer than we expected. As for me, I ended that week with the flu. Since we did not work on Sundays, my roommates went to town and bought a bottle of dark beer with which they made me a grog. It was supposed to be good against the flu. It's possible, but I had to force myself to drink it. I got over the flu, but when I think about it now, I wonder how I managed to survive since I was physically in a terrible state. It must have been due to my youth, the will to overcome obstacles, and especially the desire to survive.

CHAPTER 7

Living Conditions
at the Dam

First, I want to say that my comrades and I were shocked by the destruction caused to the dam and the neighboring valley. As I looked at the landscape around the lake, however, everything seemed so peaceful, everything evoked vacations and *joie de vivre*. Alas, all that was in the past. When I thought about it, I was filled with an immense sadness. I was asking myself if I would someday find again the possibility to enjoy in peace the beauty of nature without reservations. I would think back to the beautiful days spent on the banks of the Marne River, to swimming in it, to the peaceful evenings spent at home, and to the vacations spent in the Morvan.[1] And I missed the music so much. Fortunately, my faith helped me. I would get a grip on myself, and I offered to God the ordeal that was imposed on me by the events and by the Nazis.

Life in the camp, particularly in my barrack, was marked by a fraternal friendship. Some Sundays I would go to mass in the church of the neighboring village of Körbecke. The church was built in the baroque style and was a curiosity for me, because I was seeing this style of architecture for the first time. In my last days at the Möh-netal Dam, I attended mass in Günne, a village that was closer to my new camp. I remember that one Sunday, as it was my turn to sweep and clean our room, one of my roommates took the broom from my hands and said: "Go, go see your priest!" And he took over my chore. This fraternal gesture exemplifies the spirit that reigned among us. As for me, whose parents could not send food, I would share happily the bottle of Champagne that they could send me in rare packages. One day, one of my roommates had the idea to sus-pend the cork from the ceiling to remember this good moment.

As autumn was approaching, the Secours National Français, the French National Assistance, sent to the Todt Organization a large package of clothes that were distributed to us. I inherited a woman's green overcoat big enough for two men of my size! But the height of the comedy was what was given to a fellow nicknamed "Cauli-flower." It was a coat with tails. You had to see him shoveling dirt with his tails! Our clothing problems gave us an excuse to slow down our work as much as possible. For example, one of our work-mates, finding himself without shoes, went to the firm's office to ask for some. But, as there were none, he was given a note to exempt him from work on the construction site if he did KP in the kitchen of the camp. This was a great deal! Naturally, the next and following days saw an impressive number of fellows without shoes. Obvi-ously, I was among them. In a week, the whole camp was without shoes, even though some guys had four pairs. I remember seeing only one man going to work one morning. The policeman of the camp came again and again into my barrack looking for shoes. He never saw any trace of any! Needless to say that, after two weeks of that comedy, the supply room of the camp was crammed with clogs with wooden soles. And, of course, we had to go back on the trail to the work site. This episode demonstrates our will to resist and the creativity of our efforts to cause disorder within the system when an occasion presented itself. Indeed, we tried to multiply the occa-sions to do nothing. Sometimes, these occasions were much more serious and even dangerous. For example, several times the cable of the lift snapped. When that happened, the lift was always loaded with a small rail car full of stones or mortar, and the weight would tear off the stopping rails at the level of distribution. To our great joy, this would stop work for half a day. I always thought that these mishaps were the result of acts of sabotage, but that was never proven. The point is that these types of incidents could have produced very serious wounds to anyone close by.

Hygiene was also one of our most significant problems. In a camp like mine, lice and vermin of all sorts were always a scourge that we had to avoid. Thus, we had an imperative to keep ourselves clean. We organized ourselves to wash our clothes. In lieu of a real washing basin, we used molasses buckets, at the bottom of which we would put a piece of plank. We used the washing powder that the Todt Organization sold to us. That product washed so well that after two washes our clothes were threadbare! I had an experience one evening with a shirt: wanting to dry it, I pulled it by the collar that, without resistance, separated itself from the rest of the shirt.

The only moments when we could forget for an instant our misery were the days when we would receive mail from our families. That would warm our hearts, but often also made us shed tears. At that time, we received a salary for our work, but the Todt Organization would send it to our families through the intermediary of the Crédit Lyonnais.[2] For pocket money we got fifteen marks every month. We used this money to buy toilet soap, laundry soap, razor blades, shaving cream, and cigarettes if there were any. After we had purchased these things, there was not much left. Fortunately, our families found ways to send back to us a portion of our "salary." Like all my comrades, I was not in Germany to earn money. Like them, I considered myself a prisoner. We did not hesitate to say it when civilians would ask the question: "Is it true that you are volunteers?" We would set them straight with this answer: "No! We are forced laborers. We would prefer to be home." I believe that such statements might have made some of them think.

From time to time, when I was on the night shift, during the day I would go with a friend to one of the neighboring villages in order to buy some potatoes if we could. Most often we were refused, but we always found a person who would agree to sell us some. One day, an elderly woman made us go down in her cellar, and she asked us to take out the germinating shoots from a certain quantity of her potatoes. While we were doing this job, she told us that she had two sons in the army, one in Norway and the other in Bordeaux. She was happy that the latter was not in Russia, and she also told us that he loved France. She said that she hoped that this dirty war would end soon. When we were finished, she filled our bag and refused payment.

The Monday before Christmas 1943, I was assigned to work on the night shift. In order to have a little extra for that holiday, René Détante and I decided to make the rounds of the farms of the neighboring village. After several negative answers to our requests, a woman invited us to enter her house. She was baking cookies. In the kitchen there were also a young girl and a tall and strong young man, probably a soldier on leave. We assumed they were her children. The mother sent the girl to the cellar to fetch potatoes. She whispered some words into the ear of her son, who disappeared in an adjacent room. The girl filled our bag with potatoes. The son, coming back, gave each of us a pâté sandwich. The mother filled our pockets with cookies and did not accept a *pfennig*. Such a gesture was comforting in the context of the events we were living under and considering the hate that existed all around. These victuals were for my comrades at Christmas, for that evening I received orders to leave for Hagen the next day.

Besides these escapades in the countryside in search of potatoes, I happened once or twice, with a friend, to go to Soest—the *Kreis,* or county, seat—to do some shopping and especially to give myself a day off, without pay of course. To get there, we had to walk about six miles. I remember having gone into a shop to buy pins. I was served by a pretty young lady who had hurried toward us because we were French. As I found her beautiful, I would have loved to flirt with her, but we had to take the bus to get back to the camp. In fact, it was dangerous to try to date German girls. They and we risked prison or a camp of "reeducation through work," the infamous AEL (*Arbeitserziehungslager*) that were a bit like concentration camps. Moreover, risks aside, I thought myself hardly presentable, with my clothes in rags, to really court a pretty girl.

⟶ Near the end of October 1943, when the reconstruction of the dam's wall was completed, an inauguration ceremony took place with the participation of high dignitaries from the Todt Organization. It was a Sunday, and we had the day off. I took advantage of that to take a walk with some friends on the road that ran along the shore of the lake, a road used by the Mercedes of the dignitaries. Among them was Albert Speer, whom we caught a glimpse of in a full brown uniform.

During and after its reconstruction, the dam on the Möhne was never again bombed. However, air alerts were numerous, either because of the passage of large bomber formations flying elsewhere, or because of bombings in the area. At night, we could observe the flak shots. On the dam, anti-aircraft canons and machine guns joined in the concert of those of the whole region. We could see the sky lit up by tracer bullets. It was like a sinister firework of a tragic beauty. The noise of the shells exploding mixed with the humming of the planes, and the hundreds of spotlights sweeping the sky gave a vision of the apocalypse, a vision that I would experience again later and in greater danger.

⟶ During the six months that I spent working at the dam, I was witness to several accidents. The first involved a young guy from my camp who, wanting to bathe in the river below the dam, shattered his skull against a rock. We buried him in the cemetery of Günne, a village close to the dam. We had planned a funeral mass in the village church, but the management of the Todt Organization forbade it. The priest was only allowed to bless the body in the street. We took that to heart, and our hate of the Nazis increased.

One morning, at seven o'clock, at the time of leaving the construction site after a night of work, I was with members of my team next to the lift on the platform of our level, twenty meters above the ground. Suddenly, we heard an awful racket in the lift's cage and some yelling. A few seconds later, we saw the gang car that pushed the small rail cars crash against the pulley of the lift. At the same moment, the body of the driver fell. That gave us all quite a shock. I believe that this man was also buried in Grünne. There was also an Italian who electrocuted himself on one of the cables that anchored the scaffold. Then, a Dutch fellow was struck on the head by a plank that fell from twenty meters above him. There were other accidents that I did not witness.

At the camp, the punishments that could be inflicted on us included: (1) the *pelote*, which consisted of forcing a man to stay crouched, without his buttocks touching his heels and with a wooden log in his hands, for one hour; a guard next to him would hit him if he weakened; (2) prison; and (3) the best of the best, the "reeducation through work" camp (AEL). This last punishment was nearly as bad as a concentration camp. But we did not really understand what that meant. The AEL of the Todt Organization was in the town of Bielefeld.

The last camp I was in at the dam was overseen by a *Lagerführer* named Wolf. It was he who had had the command of our convoy from Soissons. He had an infirmity—a very pronounced clubfoot. Was it congenital, the result of a war wound, or the result of an accident?

It was surely the reason he was not at the front. All day long, he would pace up and down the camp, a machine gun slung over one shoulder, hunting laggards, accompanied by a German Shepherd dog. He was so tempted to use his machine gun that one day he killed his dog. Those were the hands into which we had been put! My suffering on the construction site of the dam and in the camps of Delecke and Möhnetal ended on Tuesday, December 21, 1943, when I was sent to Hagen in the Ruhr basin. There, other sufferings and bombings were waiting for me.

CHAPTER 8

Hagen-in-Westfalen
and Its Camps

That Tuesday, December 21, 1943, it was extremely cold. The thermometer must have indicated ten degrees Fahrenheit. In this transfer to Hagen, there were others besides me. They included Primo Coletto, an Italian mason, who must have been fifty years old; a guy from Normandy whose name I have forgotten; Torremans, the Belgian miner that we had nicknamed "Charleroi"; and a fellow not too sophisticated like the two others, one named Desdion, who came from the region of Orléans, and the fellow nicknamed "Cauliflower" whose real name I do not think I ever knew. We were put in the back of a small truck that did not have a top. We left for Hagen, which was some forty miles away. I set myself against the back of the cabin to be protected from the wind. Unfortunately, my shoulders, neck, and head were higher than the top of the cabin, and I arrived in Hagen practically frozen. It was late morning when we arrived. The town showed traces of a recent bombing. After driving through streets full of debris and ruins, we stopped near the railroad station, on Goeringstrasse to be exact, at the *Leitstelle* of the Todt Organization, that is, a transit station. This was indeed to be our situation for we were "lent," temporarily, to the telegraph service to repair the telephone lines smashed in the last bombing.

The place where we were put up was a former hotel that was half demolished. On the first floor, in what had been a lobby with a bar, cots had been installed for us. This was to be our barrack in a sense. On the upper floors there were some individual bedrooms still intact that were occupied by the *Lagerführer*, whose name was also Wolf, like our overseer at the dam, and by some French, Dutch, and German employees of the *Frontführung*, that is, the regional headquarters of the Todt Organization. Among them was Fritz, a German who was the switchboard operator, and four Frenchmen, including a barber dressed in a Todt uniform, another who served as janitor, and a fellow who worked in the kitchen that fed the workers of all the town's camps. The fourth was a strange fellow by the name of Willi. His family, which had emigrated to France in 1933 or 1934, was apparently of German Jewish origins. Willi had the role of interpreter since he spoke German perfectly. According to his intimate friends, he had several identity papers with different names. He would often go on a binge with high Todt functionaries, and, it was said, that he had made numerous feminine conquests. His false identity papers gave him the possibility to escape any compromising situation when there was some sort of control by the police.

During 1944, the *Leitstelle* hosted some Flemish workers in transit, who were back from the Russian front. One of them surprised Willi, who, thinking that he was asleep, was going through the pockets of his clothes. I never learned what happened right then, but the Flemish fellow must have complained to the *Frontführung* and Willi was interrogated several times. Curiously, his questioning was intermittent, and he would come back to the hotel every evening with no sign that he had been mistreated. Probably, the bosses with whom he had been close, and who certainly knew that he was Jewish, were embarrassed by the situation. I remember that one evening he was speaking on the telephone with a woman. She must have asked him the question: "What do I hear . . . it seems that you are Jewish?" Then, very embarrassed, he answered: "Hmm. . . . On my mother's side there were Jews in the family." Finally, one day, Willi disappeared, but I heard that someone had seen him in a hospital being treated for some illness.

The sole Dutch in the group worked in the *Frontführung*. With us there was also a young Algerian, who was to be repatriated and whom Willi never ceased to bother. He slept on the cot next to mine, and I think it was he who gave me a gift of fleas! It was thus in this place and with these people that I was to spend several weeks.

—✦— One night, shortly after my arrival, sirens began to wail *Vollalarm*—red alert! The flak guns woke me up. The noise of the explosions was so intense that I thought that bombs were falling. My fright was such that, in my hurry, I had a hard time putting my pants on before going down into the cellar.

On Friday evening, Christmas Eve, the Italian, Primo Coletto, and I decided to go back to the camp of the dam to spend the holiday with our friends. With our OT *Ausweiss*,[1] we took the train for Soest. I will never forget the welcome of our buddies as we arrived. When I knocked on the barrack door, I heard a chorus of, "It's him!" Less than a week had passed since my departure from that camp, but our joy to see each other again was as great as if we had not seen each other for months. The Champagne cork was still hanging from the ceiling as a sign of the friendship that united us. I thus spent two good days there, and it was with a heavy heart that I took the train back to Hagen on Sunday evening.

From the day I arrived at the *Leitstelle* of Hagen, my food ration, like that of my comrades, was reduced to one soup per day. A big pot of soup was brought to our room every evening from the Todt kitchen with a ration of bread. All this, as I said, was for the next twenty-four hours. Our soup ration was that of a one-liter size ladle and a piece of bread that weighed around 250 grams. We also received a slice of salami or twenty grams of artificial honey. Once a week, we were given a milk soup with a piece of sugar. However, at the beginning of our stay at the *Leitstelle*, we were not counted among the permanent personnel. As a result, we did not receive our food rations regularly. We always had to complain. Very often, Primo Coletto urged me to do so. He would say: "You speak German. You should go to the *Frontführung*. It is the turn of the French to complain!" One evening, I decided to do it. My intervention began in a somewhat comical way. I was rather nervous after having made my complaint when a *Frontführer*, passing in the corridor where I was, asked me what I was doing there. In my fright, I forgot that I spoke German and I explained to him my complaint in French. Not understanding a word I said, he sent for an interpreter. Meanwhile, the *Lagerführer* of the *Leitstelle*, also passing by, asked me what I wanted. Then he said: "But you speak German!" Regaining my wits, I mentioned again my complaint, this time in German. When he arrived, the interpreter seemed rather perplexed. Finally, I was told that a favorable response would be given to my demand. And, indeed, it was done. I must say that, not too sure of myself at first, I was rather proud of the result.

The short time I spent in this sort of camp, related to my work for the *Telegraphenamt*, the telephone and telegraph office, was the least bad of all the time I spent in the forced labor camps of Nazi Germany. However, it was the beginning of my greatest hardships and my closest contact with the realities of war.

Hunger ate at my guts more and more. Naturally, my fundamental worry—an instinctive worry, one might say—was to try to find the smallest crumbs to add to my usual menu. But these crumbs were rare!

Fights between the men of this group were exceptional. But I remember that one day, for some unknown reason, the janitor of the *Frontführung* had a fight with Fritz. As the latter came out of the fight with black eyes, the *Lagerführer* asked him the next day what had happened. Fritz simply answered that he had fallen down the stairs.

In the evenings, we all liked to gather around the stove that was in the middle of the room that served as our dormitory. I remember that I once found a wooden egg, and I used it to darn my socks—as we still had some at that time. It was not long before my buddies, seeing what I was doing, gave me their socks to darn. Next to me, another buddy would amuse himself by repairing watches. He did it with a pair of pliers and his knife. And it worked!

To our sordid life, besides the hunger, were added air alerts that became more and more frequent and which continued until our liberation.

⟶ Since the end of 1943, the Todt Organization recruited (willingly or by force, we never found out) boys to incorporate them in the *Schutz Korps*, a military group organized for defense. After a month at a German military school, the new recruits were put in charge of guarding depots or camps of Italian prisoners who worked for the Todt Organization. Some of these boys were even sent to the rear of the Russian front. They wore the Todt brown uniform with an armband with a swastika. The advantage of their situation was that they were better fed than we were. And it happened that a fellow who worked in my unit was incorporated into such a group. One evening, during the summer of 1944, he came to see me at the Boele camp where I was at that time. Before I arrived at my barrack, none of my roommates had said a word to him. A Frenchman in a German uniform was too shameful! He was to come back to see me two days later. However, he must have regained his post late, and I never saw him again. After the war, he wrote me a letter in which he said that he had ended his stay in Germany in a concentration camp. However, I never had any more news from him.[2]

In principle, we had the right to a home leave. This was something we all dreamed about. The Todt Organization had established a rule to grant us such leaves: one fellow had to vouch for the return of his workmate from his leave. For this, he had to sign a paper that said that he would be deprived of a leave if his workmate did not come back. Obviously, by the end of 1943, of all those who went on leave, none ever came back. Thus, when my friend from Normandy had managed to obtain a leave, he asked me to vouch for him. I did not hesitate to do it, but I did so with no illusions. I thought that this sacrifice was part of my Christian testimony. On this score, some fellows had devised a trick to obtain a leave. They would ask their families to send them a telegram announcing the death of a parent. That worked. As for me, I loathed to use this trick, and, in fact, very few of my friends did it.

Indeed, it was not easy to escape from the Todt Organization. I had the proof of that in the spring of 1944. Each time I was transferred from one camp to another, I would return regularly to the *Leitstelle*. One day, I had spent the noon break there as I still worked for the *Telegraphenamt*. As I was leaving, I saw the interpreter arriving accompanied by a living skeleton. I will never forget that vision. I had never seen such horror. When I came next to him, I asked: "Is that you, Lefranc?" He answered affirmatively. I then asked what had happened to him. He told me that he had tried to return to France clandestinely but that he was arrested. He had just spent three months in prison and three months in an AEL, which, the reader is reminded, was much like a concentration camp.

⟶ Near the end of January 1944, I was transferred to a camp that was installed inside an immense sports arena. It was at the end of Echeseyer Strasse, a main artery of Hagen right in the middle of an industrial zone and next to the railroad marshaling yards. This was a vast space with a high ceiling that two cast iron stoves could not heat. Since it was very cold in the morning, I would wake up feeling like an icicle. To "warm up," my friends and I would wash with cold water distributed by a pipe with holes. This pipe was outside. We had to break the ice that hung from each hole. We had all the comforts of home! The locale had a rather cosmopolitan population, but Czechs were a majority. We did not have a bomb shelter, not even a ditch. During the night alerts, which were practically every night, we would go out in a field that was behind the building. Fortunately, there was no bombing in that area.

Our little group did not stay long in that sports arena. Still working for the Hagen *Telegraphenamt*, at the beginning of March, we were ordered to move to the camp of Boeler Heide. This camp of the Todt Organization was located in a field with trees, on a hill that dominated one side of the marshaling yards and the town. It also dominated the valley of the Ruhr River and factories as well as railroad tracks. This site was called Haus Ruhreck. At the gate of the camp there was a flak battery equipped with long cannons of 105 millimeter caliber. This was part of a system of defense that we found in proximity to all Todt camps. This, in a sense, made targets out of us. The *Lagerführer* was naturally a German, but he had a Dutch aide whose first name was Jan. He was a Todt member and thus wore the brown uniform with an armband with a swastika. He was even nastier than his superior.

The camp was populated in large part by Flemish and Italians. At that time, there was only one barrack for the French. My team and I reached that camp at night after walking two miles or so, even though where we came from was only five hundred yards away. Since it was late when we arrived, everybody was asleep. As we were dead tired, we slept on the floor of the first barrack that we found. The next morning, I found there some buddies who had worked at the dam: Raoul Angot, Régis Bruyère, Charles Filloux, a certain Richard, and the Corsican Casanova, who had been a sailor assigned to a submarine, and others whose names I have forgotten. There was also André Geerts from Bruyères-et-Montbérault, who was a former seminarian. It was with him that I was to become a member of the clandestine JOC group.[3] We remained together until the end of the war, and our relationship was always to be marked by great fraternity. We suffered together at work; we suffered from hunger together; we were afraid together; and we sustained the danger of bombings together.

Several days after our arrival, we moved to another barrack at the other end of the camp; it was occupied by Frenchmen. It is among them that we got to know Jacques Prévot, a young priest, deported as we were. It is with him that we created the JOC group, and it was he who gave us the spiritual comfort that we needed so much. I remember the celebration of Easter 1944 and my confession to him in the alleys of the camp in the moonlight. That Sunday, we celebrated the Holy Mass in the chapel of the hospital that was nearby. We really felt close to Christ at that moment! Still today, I believe that God helped me overcome my fears and the harshness of the life that was imposed upon us. It is from Him that we received the motivation for our *Jocist* action. He helped us to carry our cross, share the suffering of our comrades, and prove to them that faith gives strength and serenity in the worst times of our lives. We had to be worthy of Him. Each morning, we offered our day to the Lord, making the sign of the cross, and praying in these terms: "My God, don't let us die of a violent or unforeseen death; do not permit that I die without having received the holy sacrament." In the evening, again after making the sign of the cross, we placed our night in His hands. Indeed, these nights were often disrupted and full of danger, especially after the beginning of the summer of 1944. I remember that a day after the bombing of the region one of my comrades hailed me and said: "Say, Elie, there are some who did not make the sign of the cross this morning!"

The vicar of the Boele parish, who was also the chaplain of the hospital next to our camp, indirectly participated in our religious life. It was he who permitted us to celebrate mass, with Father Prévot, in the hospital chapel. I never had real contacts with this German priest, but I still remember the look of his eyes when we met him: he expressed a deep sadness. I have always had the impression that he was asking for our forgiveness. Another German priest had let be known his admiration for the young French Christians. He said to one of my *Jocist* comrades: "I wish so much that the young of Germany acted in this way!"

Every Sunday, André Geerts and I left the camp at the same time as others were going to work. We would attend the parish mass. Afterward, we would go to town where we wandered the rest of the day. (I must say that, as long as I worked at the *Telegraphenamt*, this did not pose a problem for me.) Thus, we went once or twice to the movies. But the fear of bombings led us to avoid that type of recreation. Sometimes, we would enter a pub to drink a beer while listening to music, for fairly often there was an orchestra in these establishments.

At that time, perhaps for security purposes or more likely for propaganda, we were issued an arm band with the inscription "Arbeitet für O.T." and a number as well as a sort of dog tag with a number, the significance of which I never understood and that I always thought was bogus—but no name! It was in fact totally useless for identification. While I kept the dog tag around my neck for a few days, I never once wore the arm band.

CHAPTER 9

Work at the *Telegraphenamt* of Hagen

On December 22, 1943, I began my work at the *Telegraphenamt* with other workmates. In this job, the human contacts were completely different from those I had with my overseers from the Todt. At the *Telegraphenamt*, my boss was a fine man in his sixties. His name was Herr Brüne. Since he was a civil servant, he had to be a member of the Nazi party. But this man was far from being a veritable Nazi, with everything that this word meant. I quickly realized that fact. At one point, he had lost his party pin that he regularly wore on his jacket. He was very worried about that. But, one day, he was wearing it again. The Italian mason, Primo Coletto, asked him: "Eh boss, you found your pin?" Herr Brüne answered: "Yes, and I am very happy about it because of *diese Bande*!" This word *Bande* in German had, usually, a pejorative meaning. For Herr Brüne, the Nazis were no more than a band of thugs.

Herr Brüne ardently wished for the end of the war and the return of peace. He knew very well that it could only take place with the defeat of Germany. I remember that, on the morning of June 6, 1944, as I was working in a large underground junction box in the railroad freight station of Hagen, I saw him arrive with a smile on his face. He bent down above the opening of the box and, noticing that I was alone, he told me: "Poulard! The Americans are arriving! They are in Rouen!" He was very happy! Of course, he was wrong about how far the Allies had gotten that day, but he wanted me to enjoy this good news, share his joy, and have hope. This man, who had never wanted war, one day confided in me: "I have only a daughter, and I am glad about that; she will not go to war."

That evening in the barrack the talk was only about the Allies' landing in Normandy. The enthusiasm was such that we saw ourselves home for Christmas, even though I remember having made the remark that we needed to be prepared for very hard times before we could have this great joy. I said that we would certainly be subjected to severe bombings. One of my comrades retorted naively: "They will be careful not to hit us." My answer to this hope was: "Do you believe that they can see us from so high? It will be better for us to take care of ourselves!" Someone then made this statement: "You! You really raise up our spirits!" But, unfortunately, I was right.

At the end of June, as André Geerts and I were taking a walk in Hagen, we passed in front of a concert hall where a show was being put on to French workers. Learning that, we went in and saw this performance given by a troupe of French prisoners. These prisoners had been "transformed" into "free workers"—free in the sense the Nazis gave to this word. In that troupe, there was an orchestra. After the spectacle, I asked whether there was room for another saxophone. The musicians were very happy to meet me. They gave me the address of the place where they played, which had been appointed to them by the Arbeitsamt (the German work agency), an organization of the Nazi party that controlled and kept watch on, among other things, the entertaining of groups of foreign workers. One evening, after my work (I was still for a few more days at the *Telegraphenamt*), I went to that locale, which was in the theater of a café named Nordpol. There I met the whole troupe. The actors were directed by a former variety artist, a certain Geo Montax, who had a repertoire similar to that of Georgius, a famous pre-war French entertainer. There were two girls in the troupe: Jeannette, who was French and a comedian and a singer, and Suzanne, who was Belgian and who sang opera arias. The latter claimed to have sung at the Théâtre de la Monnaie in Brussels. It is true that she sang very well. But, having no respect for volunteers, I kept a reserved attitude toward these two girls.

The director of the orchestra was named Duchesne. As I said before, the whole group was made up of "transformed" prisoners of war. Their musical instruments had been sent by the French "aid to the prisoners" services. I was thus incorporated into the saxophone section and was given a C melody saxophone, a rather rare instrument.

No need to describe the ambiance in my barrack when I brought that instrument to the camp. Naturally, I played my repertoire. My buddies tapped on their mess kits to accompany me. In such moments, we would forget our misery, and we got beyond our situation of slaves.

Once a week, I would go to the Nordpol to rehearse with the orchestra. Periodically, we gave concerts or theatrical performances in camps of deported workers. One evening, as we were playing in one of these camps, the sirens blew the daily air alert. All the Germans went down in the shelter, but we, taken up by the whirling of the sounds and rhythms of our music, continued to play. When we stopped, we could hear the humming of the planes above our heads. Fortunately, there was no bombing in our sector that evening!

One Sunday, we went as far as Iserlohn in a tram so we could give a show in a camp. Thus, I missed work that day. It was fall, and the region that we passed through had traces of recent bombings. There were ruins as far as one could see. At the end of the journey, we were alone with the conductor of the tram. Very naturally, we began to sing (a musician always has a tune in his head, even in the worst moments of life). I will always remember the great sadness of the conductor when he told us: "Bitte, singen Sie doch nicht!"[1] His tone was almost imploring, so we stopped.

The evenings of rehearsals, I would leave the camp after having eaten my soup and washed up, including washing my tin. I came back to my bed around midnight, and I still had to get up at five in the morning. This was an added strain for my body to pay, but it was a way to keep my morale and my dignity, despite my sad physical state. This continued until the beginning of December 1944. At that time, we had to stop all our activities because the bombings were more and more numerous, and moving around had become too risky and even impossible at night.

—✦— Among the personnel of the *Telegraphenamt*, there were some German specialists who reconnected the telephone lines. I remember only the first name of one of them: Willi. He was something over thirty years old and had a large family. He was drafted into the army in the fall of 1944. A small number of Luxemburgers were also employed by this state company. They were very nice to me and my French workmates. There was also a team of drivers including Karl, an old patriot with whom I had frequent discussions. Another fat fellow, a veteran of World War I, conversed often with me. When I told him that I was from the Champagne region, he related to me his souvenirs of the Great War. He told me that he had known a woman from Cumières in 1914, when the German army occupied that area. He was a rather nice man. And then there was a member of the S.A.[2] I saw him leave a few times on a motorcycle in his uniform when there was a meeting of the Nazi party in Dortmund that included high party leaders or even Hitler himself. I cannot say whether he was a bad man, for he was never arrogant with me or my workmates. However, I kept a suspicious attitude towards him.

In contrast with the Todt work sites, at the *Telegraphenamt* we did not work on Saturday afternoons or on Sundays. This was the reason I took to the habit of going to the parish mass in Boele, besides the clandestine masses. As I mentioned earlier, it was during this short period when I worked at the *Telegraphenamt* that left me the least bad memories of my forced time in Germany during the war. As an unskilled worker, my job, as well as that of my workmates, consisted in clearing up the conduits in the ruins into which telephone lines passed. In digging, it happened that I put my hands on blocks of concrete still hot several weeks after a bombing. We would clean the bricks and, after the clearing of debris, we would redo the trenches with picks and shovels. Once that was done, we would put down the ducts into which the telephone cables were to pass. Primo Coletto was in charge of the masonry of the underground conjunction boxes. In this work, I was often alone with him, who, besides his native language, also spoke German. He was not such a bad fellow, but I would anger him very much when I would spoil his mortar. For him, that mortar was always too thick or too thin, or too wet or too dry, but never good. I must confess that I did my best to really spoil everything that I could! My incompetence was such that, most of the time, he had to redo my work. As the genuine Italian that he was, he would use all the loudest swearwords of his repertoire. When the boxes were finished, we would pour some tar on the covers. I favored this work because it was not tiring.

Sometimes we would install telephones in private homes. We would dig trenches outside, then make holes in the walls of the cellars with an iron bar. We would pass the cables through the holes and fix them on concrete walls or on old plaster. Two workers did each job. One of us would stretch the cable, and the other would fix the collars, which inevitably were not to hold for very long. The nails did not penetrate very far into the concrete, which was hard. In the plaster, which was too soft or which would disintegrate, the nails barely held. In either case, it was the number of collars that assured a rather temporary fastening. This work in private homes could have some compensation. One day, when Coletto and I were digging a trench to install a telephone in an old lady's house, she brought us little pieces of white bread. The next day, she brought us some more in her cellar. She explained that she was discreet in doing so because, the day before, some people who were in the shop across the street had made some negative remarks. If that had been passed on to certain persons, she could have been in some serious trouble.

Sometimes, we would salvage some lead cables from the walls of houses in ruin. To do that, we would double the ladders to three or four meters and block them in the loose stones. This was rather unstable. Fortunately for me, because of my work at the dam, I had conquered my fear of heights.

More often, we were in cellars. The textile industry was one of the main activities in the city of Hagen, and I remember having spent quite a bit of time in the cellars of a textile factory damaged by bombs. In this clothes factory, there was a whole group of pretty young girls. When one or another would come near me, she would readily talk to me. However, I never wanted to start flirting. Besides, this was *streng verboten*, strongly forbidden, and was severely punished if caught. But my workmate Coletto dated one of them, who made him a feather pillow. In his case, he was Italian and thus considered a citizen of an allied country. Furthermore, he had come willingly to Germany several years earlier. One morning when I was doing some acrobatics on the ledge of a window to unhook a lead cable, one of these young girls, who was below in the yard next to Herr Brüne, said to him expressing her fear: "He is going to fall! He is going to fall!" Herr Brüne reassured her in his slightly nasal voice: "No, he is used to this!" I was rather proud to be the object of such solicitude. I had other occasions to be near young German girls. Since I lived at the Boele camp, I went to my work on the *Strassenbahn*, or tramway. As I liked to ride it on its platform, I would find myself near young girls who went to high school or to work, including two whom I met every morning. It was rather pleasant, but again, I never wanted to make the merest suggestion of flirtation. I looked at love as a matter much more serious. That was it! Some smiles, some demonstrations of sympathy on the part of these young girls gave a little charm and light in the grayness of my life.

All in all, in Hagen, I worked on many different sites. Thus, I moved around in all the corners of the city, which I got to know very well. And, as I have already said, I often found myself alone with a group of German specialists. I remember that, one morning, Willi tried to teach me how to do the connections of telephone lines. He explained to me the way to twist the very fine wires of each line, but he did not continue the lessons. I believe that some of his colleagues dissuaded him from do so, fearing sabotage.

Among the sites where I worked were the cellars of the city police. These were under the headquarters of all the police forces of Hagen, including the Gestapo. It was always the same work: to place cables at the top of walls or under ceilings. The "care" that I gave to this job was always the same: that is, those cables could not be pulled too hard after I had attached them! As it happened, it was at that location on one Saturday morning that Herr Brüne said to me: "Poulard, please don't go too fast because, if you finish before noon, I will have to send you to another work site." That day, I had to prepare plaster to fix the receivers. But I did it in such a way that I spoiled the plastering very well. In the end, a policeman did the work for me! And, in the course of the morning, a man in civilian clothes came to me to ask in perfect French with a Parisian accent:

"You wouldn't have some plaster to give me?" Some other police-men intervened to castigate him for asking such a question. They told him that I might not have enough for the job I was doing. I be-lieve that this "civilian" was probably a member of the Gestapo try-ing to entrap me. One morning that Herr Brüne was leading us to the same work site several days after D-Day, one of the policemen asked him: "Herr Brüne, what do you think of the military situation in the West?" I laughed inside when I heard the hypocritical reply of Herr Brüne: "It's OK. Things must stay as they are and positions must be held."

—◆— During these six months at the *Telegraphenamt*, as I said above, I worked in all corners of the city of Hagen and for different people. It was thus that one morning I was alone digging a trench to bring a telephone line to a bungalow occupied by some SS men, who sported on their caps a skull-and-bones insignia. A young SS man was there, sitting on the low wall of the fence, looking at what I was doing. As I would rest after every second time I hit the ground with my pick axe, the work was not moving fast. After a while, ir-ritated, the SS man began to shout at me some strong "Schneller!" "Faster!" Because that had no effect on me, a moment later, he asked me in a brutal tone: "Bist du krank?" "Are you sick?" Finally, see-ing that inertia was the only force I was using, he pushed me away and took the pick from my hands and did all the digging. All I had to do was to clean up the debris behind with a shovel. That was not so hard!

Another day, I had to clean up the debris from an underground conjunction box damaged by a flak shell that had not exploded in the air but had fallen back down, exploding in the middle of the city, killing one person. Thus, I had to move bloody rubble. It smelled like fresh eggs. I was going to smell that odor often during the months I still had to spend in Germany.

Several times, I went to Dortmund with some *Telegraphenamt* employees to deliver empty cable drums. Some were very big. They were placed on a trailer hitched to a truck. I was given a thick fur coat and motorcyclist goggles. I was put on the high seat at the head of the trailer where I would serve as the brake man. I must say that the fur coat was not superfluous because it was very cold. During the trip, I would look at the sky for any sight of bombers. However, on these trips we did not encounter any problems. As we used bricks for certain jobs, it happened once that I had to enter an open oven. I was given some special gloves to handle the extremely hot bricks. And the heat in the oven was incredible!

If my work conditions at the *Telegraphenamt* were, in a sense, acceptable, the food was still that of the Todt, that is, soup once per day. One time at noon, I was taking my break at the workshop with my workmates Torremans and Cauliflower. Herr Brüne happened to pass by. He asked why we were not going to eat. We answered that at the Todt we ate only once a day. He came out with a resounding "Scheisse!" and then left. A while later, we saw him coming back carrying a bucket. This bucket contained *Hering Salat*, herring salad. It was a sort of mush of herring and red cabbage. It had a purple color. Today, that would make me want to puke. But, on that day, we rushed to it as only the famished would. How to explain what I felt at that moment, as a witness to this gesture on the part of a man who hailed from this evil people of Germany? So, yes, among those that we considered barbarous, there were people like Herr Brüne, men with a heart.

When we were at the workshop at the time of an alert, we would run to a four-story bunker that was in a nearby avenue. It was a very solid shelter. It had thick walls of reinforced concrete and was compartmented into small cells with all the comforts, including toilets. Unfortunately, we could not go there very often and, when it was possible, we had to stay in the hallways. When we were on a work site in town, we would seek shelter in a cellar, or anywhere. Fortunately, during this period, there were no heavy bombings of the city.

—✦— At the end of June 1944, the members of my team were recalled to the Todt work sites, except for Coletto, who remained as a specialist mason. As for me, I stayed with him. I believe that it was because Herr Brüne had tried to keep me in his employ. However, at the beginning of July, the Todt Organization requested me back. One evening, Herr Brüne let me know of it and told me that he had tried to keep me. That same evening, as I was coming down the tramway to get back to the camp, I found myself face to face with Herr Schwartz, the director of the firm into which I was incorporated. He called to me, in German of course, with the question: "Is it you who works at the *Telegraphenamt*?" I answered in the affirmative. Schwartz then said: "Tomorrow, Dortmund!" I retorted: "At the *Telegraphenamt*, nobody told me anything." And as the tramway was leaving, Schwartz repeated: "Tomorrow, Dortmund!" Then, angry, I yelled back at him in French: "Et, merde!" He understood me very well.

The next morning, as I arrived at the workshop, Herr Brüne came to tell me that I had to go to the Todt work site at the Dortmund-South station. I believe that he had tears in his eyes as his tone was so sad. Naturally, I shared his sadness, not only because I had to return to work for the Todt Organization, but because Herr Brüne and I had developed a real mutual friendship. He knew what I thought, and he wished ardently the end of the abject regime under which he lived and the end of that war whose conclusion he could imagine.

CHAPTER 10

Life at the Boeler
Heide Camp

When I was reassigned to work at the Dortmund-South station in July 1944, I still lived in the Boeler Heide camp where the "infamous" Jan, the Dutch aide to the camp's *Lagerführer*, became my personal enemy. While I worked for the *Telegraphenamt*, I was often alone with German workers and thus was obliged to speak their language all day. That led me to make great progress in German. I was able to express myself without an accent and with a decent vocabulary. Such proficiency in the language turned out to be very useful for me and permitted me to help my comrades. Every time there was a complaint to be made, naturally it was I that was put in charge to make it. My buddies would tell me: "You speak the lingo, go do it!" Even though I was not very bold, I did it. Every time, it was Jan that I faced. Since, in general, he would receive me badly, I would lose my temper and that gave me courage. The discussion would end up being rather hot, but I would win the case. I remember in particular one complaint about our sugar ration that we had not been getting for several weeks.

I ended up being quite disliked by this Jan, so much so that, every time that he was mad at us, it was I whom he addressed. For example, during an air raid, at the moment the Allied planes were passing over us, there was always some joker who put something to burn in the stove. Of course, that made sparks going up the chimney. Then, Jan would rush into our barrack, and I was the one bawled out with curse words. He would pour any liquid he could find into the stove. In the fall of 1944, some buddies warned me that he had said that before the Allies arrived he would kill some of us. They added: "Be careful; you are likely to be among them!" Luckily for me, at the end of the war, I was in another camp.

There is no doubt that this Jan had me in his sights. The anecdote below proves that he took advantage of any occasion to vex me. As I already mentioned, since I was in Hagen, I did not have to work on Sundays. As long as I worked for the *Telegraphenamt*, this was normal for me. However, on the Todt construction sites, people worked seven days a week. But many of my buddies also took Sunday off, more or less regularly, without asking anyone's permission!

In August 1944, Hitler declared the *Total Einsatz*, that is, the total effort for the war. This new policy affected us doubly because, from that day on, our salaries were no longer sent to our families. We were told that they were frozen at the Deutsche Bank. Obviously, when we heard this news, we did not harbor any illusions. In fact, these salaries are apparently still frozen since that time. But I repeat, for me and all other Frenchmen, we did not care, for we were not in Germany to earn money. We considered ourselves captives and not workers at the service of the Third Reich.

Thus, the first Sunday of the *Total Einsatz*, the Flemish, having heard that they would no longer be paid, did not go to work. Several guys from my barrack, those who were not at their first dominical absence, did the same. That evening, at soup time, the bread ration, usually for two days, was reduced to that of one day for those who had not worked. Some of my friends thus found themselves with a half ration. By chance, I received my full ration, but one of my punished comrades told me that Jan wanted to see me with my rations. I knew right away what that meant. I borrowed the half ration of a friend and went to see my personal enemy while complaining: "Why is it that we got only a half ration?" Jan answered: "Because you did not work this Sunday!" I retorted: "Why should we work on Sundays? It's only at the Todt that people work on Sundays!" On that, I went back to my barrack, happy to have played a good trick on Jan. But that was not the end of it. The next evening, before we got our rations, at the time to queue up for soup, Jan grouped together some Flemish and me aside. He then marched us into a room that served as a prison to spend the night. We were seventeen altogether in a narrow room. All night long, we could not lie down for lack of space, and we had to remain crouched. Furthermore, we did not have our coats on, and it was cold. I can still see the faces of my friends behind the window of our barrack looking at us being escorted by Jan, his rifle slung over his shoulder. They waited for what might happen next before getting their soup. They all manifested their solidarity by putting a small portion of their soup into my mess-tin. That made it possible for me the next morning to calm down my hunger before returning to work. It is always with great emotion that I think back at that fraternal gesture. The soup was cold, but there was great warmth emanating from that selfless act of sharing! It was with great relief that I came out of the prison and into the fresh air that morning. I must confess that I was afraid for a while that more severe punishments might be given and that perhaps even an "example" might be made!

⚓ By that time, it had been already several months since our little JOC group had been put together. We would meet regularly behind the barracks of the camp. We would prepare the masses that we celebrated from time to time in the hospital chapel. We did that discreetly, for it was not authorized. We would give each other news of the latest events that took place in the various construction sites, and we reflected on the way we had lived these events as Christians. We discussed what our conduct should be in the future and how we should show our solidarity with our comrades at work as well as in the barracks. At one point, we decided to recite the rosary during air alerts and bombings. This decision was passed along to all the devoted Christians who were in Germany. We also talked about the means we could employ to participate in the defeat of Germany. At work, we were to work as slowly as possible and to break tools if possible. We also had to demoralize those on the other side when we had the occasion to talk to them. But working slowly was our best asset, and we sometimes betted against each other as to who would do nothing all day. Thus, we emphasized our solidarity with our comrades. During the summer, our JOC group got larger, so much so that, one evening, we decided to meet in the café that was located below the camp. Since we were ten or so, we put tables together. The café owner and his clients observed what we were doing with a questioning look. To avoid any problem, we decided not to renew the experience.

In the previous spring, I had received two or three packages from my parents. They were not very big because my family was suffering enormously from all sorts of shortages. However, these packages added a little to my everyday fare. A bottle of Champagne was always included. Where my parents lived, there was no shortage of that! These packages contained some packs of biscuits called *casse croûte*.[1] These were obtained by my parents with bread ration tickets received from the wife of a baker from the Aube department whom my mother had taken in during the evacuation. Indeed, these packages were very welcome.

From another quarter, since I still went back often enough to the *Leitstelle*, I had kept friendly relations with the fellow who worked in the Todt kitchens. Thus, when I got my ration of cigarettes, which was not always the case every month, I would exchange a pack for one or two bread balls. The amount of bread depended on the name on the pack or the quality of the cigarettes. I also did that for others. I must say that this was not always possible, but, when it was, the bread helped me to cling to life and to share a little.

One day, I received a package from the Chalon family of Saint-Honoré-les-Bains. What a package! It contained a lot of good things: Ovaltine, concentrated milk, saccharine, flour. Of course, I could not help but share. Unfortunately, the Chalons learned of my address very late from my sister Rolande, who was in the Nièvre department for her health.[2] I had not thought to write to them before. They wrote later to say that they had sent me another package, but I never received it. Then, Paris and France were liberated, and that cut us off completely from our families and friends.

At Pentecost 1944, I had made another trip to the Möhnetal Dam. With my Todt *Ausweiss* in my pocket, I was able to take the train. On my journey I encountered no problem, and it was with joy that I found myself again with my buddies who were still at the dam. Many had already been dispersed into other Todt camps in the Ruhr, and some had even been sent to the island of Helgoland. I spent again two days that I could qualify as wonderful if there had not been the drama of the war in the background. The weather was splendid. The lake was now full. My friends and I decided to take a walk around it, using the bridge at Delecke. We were trying to enjoy the present instant and forget our fears about the future. The sunny countryside looked like a vacation spot. My God, we could breathe its peace! I would have loved to continue to live in this atmosphere. My return was also without incident and, in fact, was rather pleasant. I traveled in the company of a group of young women, agents of the Reichsbahn (the German railroad). When the train left, they were in the compartment next to mine. They were singing together as a choir with different voices. One of their songs has remained in my memory: "O mia bella Napoli." Having noticed my presence, they came into my compartment. Very gently, they asked me a bunch of questions about where I was from, what I was doing, and whether I was a volunteer worker. I could see that they were very curious to know, and I took pleasure in talking with them. I do not quite remember what I told them, but to their last question, I made it clear to them that, like my comrades, I had been deported.

The summer of 1944 was very warm. This caused a proliferation of parasites in our bedding: fleas especially but also lice if we were lax with our body hygiene. In all the camps to which we were sent, our beds were double bunks with thin mattresses of straw on top of wooden planks. We often got rid of these mattresses because of the vermin inside them. In my case, I had a sleeping bag that my mother had made out of bed sheets. Every evening, I would take it outside, turn it inside out, and shake it to expel the hundreds of fleas that were in it. As for lice, when we found some, we had to put our underwear in boiling water and wash ourselves thoroughly—in cold water of course. It happened that, in a barrack, one fellow did not have the courage to keep himself clean. His roommates took him to the bank of the Ruhr and washed him with a scrubbing brush. That was harsh, but the health of the whole barrack was at stake. Typhus was waiting for us. I must say that the sanitary installations of our camps were more than spartan! The "bathroom" was located at the end of an ensemble of barracks-dormitories. It was equipped with round cement basins. The taps gave only cold water, and this room was not heated. No need to describe our contortions when we "showered" under these taps. It was there that I came out with my repertoire of opera arias and other songs. Some of my comrades came to that room just to listen to me. The latrines were a simple ditch, three or four yards long. It was about two yards deep and had a tin roof. At the edge of the ditch and on its whole length, there was a beam. It was on this beam that we would sit to do our needs. It was not comfortable, but we were used to worse. When there were several of us there, you can imagine the sight! For hygiene, it happened once or twice that we had to go through a disinfection station. Our body hair was daubed with some sort of disinfectant, and our clothes were put in a sterilizer. But that was not enough to definitely rid us of our parasites.

CHAPTER 11

Dortmund-South Work Site

At the beginning of July 1944, I was back working on Todt sites. I was assigned to the firm Wiemer and Trachte, which was in charge of repairing the marshaling yards of the Dortmund-South station. These had been badly damaged during a recent bombing. Thus, my team was assigned to fix railroad tracks. This meant putting rails in place on stamped steel ties in the form of an upside down U. The ballast had to be pushed under the ties to stabilize them. For me, as for my workmates, the trick was to pretend to push very hard and to make sure that the stones did not go under the ties. Another of our tricks was to not really tighten the splice bars. As a result, after the passage of the first locomotive, the track would sag a bit, forming some gracious undulations, and the work had to be done over again. That slowed down putting the tracks back in service. Because of our actions, the Todt would bring in other teams—Russians most of the time, men or women.

I was also part of a team that worked on the reconstruction of a switching tower. At one point, we had to cement the top floor. To do that, the concrete had to be brought up in tubs that masons called *oiseaux*.[1] We had to lift these tubs onto our shoulders and climb the ladder while holding them by a handle located underneath in front. With our wooden-soled shoes, that was not easy. And, as I had never done this, the first time I brought up one of these tubs, I held it by its brim in a position that was pulling me backwards. I ultimately managed to hold a tub properly. However, I asked the fellow who filled the *oiseaux* to put only one shovel-full of concrete in mine. "You are going to get in trouble," he said to me. I replied: "Don't worry about that; one shovel is enough for me!" Obviously, when I emptied my tub into the form, an overseer lashed out: "Was ist das? Es gibt nichts darin!" "What's this? There is nothing in here!" I replied to him in German: "It's enough for me; I am not a mason, I am a pharmacist!" And I continued with the same rhythm. My workmates were totally astonished.

On that work site, fearing that we might not get any soup in the evening, my friend André Geerts and I would go to a little restaurant that we had discovered that would sell meals without tickets. It was called Stammgericht. I remember that one evening, after the first dish, we called on a different waiter, who took away our dishes but left us our spoons and who brought us another *Stamm*—another dish not needing a ticket. After having eaten it, we put our spoons in our pockets, and we continued our little game with other waiters five or six times. Before leaving, we paid only for our beers! Of course, this ruse could not last, for we were not the only ones to play it.

—✦— As I said before, the summer of 1944 was very warm. On the railroad tracks, we suffered enormously from the torrid heat and from thirst, in addition to hunger. Some of my workmates worked shirtless. Of course, they got sunburns that made them suffer more, especially at night, keeping them from sleeping. I remember that our thirst was such that we drank the water coming out of the hose, covered with cement, that we used to mix the concrete.

To get to that work site from the Boele camp, we took the tram to the Herdecke station, where a special train, a *Sonderzug*, would bring us directly to the Dortmund-South station. When we came out of the tram, we would all rush to the special train to be sure to get a seat. When I had the luck to get a seat, I would sleep until the train stopped. During my work days at this site, I happened to have some contacts with employees of the Reichsbahn. One day, one of them whispered in my ear: "In Germany, there are also good people. It's only the National-Socialists who are bad." That reminded me about the old guy who, on the dam, had proclaimed: "Léon Blum, prima!"

One summer afternoon, Allied planes conducted a raid on a city of the region. As we were on alert, I found myself next to an air raid shelter with some Germans. We could see the formations of bombers pass by on the horizon. We counted them—two hundred, three hundred—and they continued to pass. The Germans there were saying: "What are our flyers doing? Are they enjoying themselves at some bar?" I remarked to them that, in 1940, it had been the same in France. My remark did not get any comment.

—✦— As the earlier work site of our firm had been in the freight yards of Hagen, we had to transport all the supplies from there to Dortmund either by rail or by truck. Several times, I had the job of loading rail cars or trucks. One day, I was with my team loading a freight car when I noticed that it was starting to roll away. Knowing that some Russians were working on the track not far away, I ran after the car to get to its brake. However, in my way, there was a sort of fence that I jumped over. When I reached the ground on the other side, I felt it giving way under me. I had dived into an old latrine that had been covered up and enclosed. No need to describe in what state I found myself. My pants, made of wood fibers, were impregnated with excrement where maggots teemed. I tried to clean myself under a water hose to no avail. My clothes continued to emit an awful and persistent stink, and that persuaded my overseer to send me back to camp. There, I threw away my pants and my wooden shoes. These, however, were replaced only with half clogs that made me suffer enormously because my ankles were covered in sores.

On the last day of that job, we loaded the rest of the material on a truck. There was so much of it that the truck was overloaded. Halfway to our destination, at Löttringhausen, going up a slope, suddenly, flames shot up behind the truck's cab. My workmates and I were already rejoicing about the incident, hoping that everything would burn. Our German overseers were beside themselves! Unfortunately as far as we were concerned, the truck had stopped in front of the entrance of a plant where there was water. And, despite our deliberately slow pace in passing the buckets of water, our overseers managed to put out the fire.

My comrades and I tried our best to never miss an occasion to do as little as possible. For example, during the summer, my ears got infected. I thus went to the *revier*, the infirmary. The doctor was not there, and I had to come back the next day. That day, the doctor sent me to see a specialist in Schwerte, a neighboring small town. The specialist was also absent when I arrived to see him! As it turned out, my infection cured itself. But these comings and goings to see doctors gave me six days of rest for a health problem that cured itself. Another time, claiming that I was susceptible to bronchitis, I was sent to an office, where a Frenchman worked, to ask for a ticket for a flannel undershirt that would protect my chest. I obtained the ticket, and I took the train with my friend Torremans to the supply warehouse of the Todt. This warehouse was located in Dahl, a village some six miles from Hagen. For me, this was another day taken away from the enemy! When we got off the train, we met a woman who was carrying a rather heavy basket. We proposed to help her, and she accepted. Of course, we hoped for some kind of compensation in the form of a piece of bread or something else to eat. In the end, however, she simply thanked us.

Considering our diet and our physical conditions, the state of our health was rather poor. Every time I could do it, I used my state of health to gain some time away from these forced work sites. I must say that it was best to avoid Todt doctors or nurses, who would send me back to work while calling me lazy. My knowledge of the German language helped me in many instances. At one time, I had a small problem with my teeth. It was not very painful, but it permitted me to steal another day off. Of course, I had to put on an act; I would grimace with pain as if I were indeed in great pain. However, I obtained the permission to see a dentist. The dentist I saw only daubed my gums with a solution with a base of tincture of iodine. When I was with him, sirens began to wail, announcing an air alert. He dismissed me quickly so he could run to a shelter. There were other hours lost on the work sites where we came up with imaginative ways to slow the progress of any project. This was our way to participate in the defeat of the Nazis. With physical pain caused by very hard work while living in primitive conditions, and with hunger, always hunger, these three summer months passed by.

—⚔— Near the end of September 1944, the Dortmund-South station was packed with railroad cars loaded with potatoes. The police guarded this treasure very tightly. However, between two patrols, we would manage to sneak into the cars to steal a few spuds. Policemen would come regularly through our barracks looking for loot. Of course, they never found anything. We took infinite precautions to hide our loot, for, if we were caught, it would mean prison or an *Arbeitsstraflager*, a hard labor camp. Thus we never brought these potatoes back to our barracks; we kept them well-hidden on the work site. And then, a few days later, Allied planes cooked them for us!

October 6, 1944, is one unforgettable date that marked my exile. That evening, Dortmund suffered a terrible bombing. The next day, we found our work site in the marshaling yards completely devastated. For example, a pile of wood that had been four meters high had been reduced to a few inches of ashes. The work site sheds were burned up, and only the steel of the tools that had been in them was left on the ground. When my workmates and I arrived at our own shed, we found it basically gone, but we found the bucket in which we had hidden potatoes. These were really cooked! Then, we all sat down on the ground and feasted on potatoes. Smoke from the fires surrounded us. All around us, everything was in ruins. It was a spectacle of such devastation that one of our overseers exclaimed: "Ein Totenfeld!" "A field of death!" We, as French forced laborers, had a mixed reaction. We rejoiced about the disaster that had hit our enemies, but we also feared to be victims as well one day.

We took advantage of the surrounding chaos to do nothing all day. And, since there were several air alerts that day, we spent most of our time in a bunker. As I had learned from my father, a veteran of World War I, when the danger of a bombing seemed to approach, I would put the lapel of my coat between my teeth. My father had told me that doing so would avoid a potential internal hemorrhage that could be caused by the explosions. The next day, my friends and I were going to see greater horrors.

CHAPTER 12

Dortmund *Hauptbahnhof* after October 6, 1944

On October 6, 1944, before the sirens began to wail, we heard the noise of formations of flying fortresses passing above our camp at Boeler Heide. We learned later that there was a total of 850 planes. Hearing the infernal humming produced by all these planes together, we came out of the barrack, and we got ready to enter the trench that served as our bomb shelter. We then heard the sirens howl, and, at the same time, the ground shook under our feet. Bombs were falling on Dortmund. From where we were we could see the flashes of the explosions and of the incendiary sticks. Then, after a moment, all we could see was just smoke. The explosions of the bombs, the raging shots of the flak, the sky illuminated by hundreds of spotlights, all that had the feel of apocalypse.[1]

The next morning, since my work site was in Dortmund, we were thrust into horror: a city of 600,000 inhabitants in ruins, fires everywhere, hundreds of dead bodies in the streets, and the odor of fresh blood mixed with that of burned flesh. The next day, Sunday, October 8, my workmates and I were sent to the main railroad station of Dortmund—the *Hauptbahnhof*. To get to it, we had to walk through the rubble of destroyed apartment buildings that lay all around. In fact, the streets had for all practical purposes disappeared. They were covered with pieces of walls, bricks, burning furniture, shreds of curtains, and again that odor of burned flesh and fresh blood. It was unbearable.

Here and there, a sign indicated an unexploded bomb, a *Blindgänger*. On our way to the *Hauptbahnhof*, there was a church whose four walls remained standing. The roof was gone, and the windows were all destroyed. Through the large gaping holes on all sides, a large crucifix could be seen still suspended in the middle of the nave. Thus, we could see Christ every time we passed by this church on our way to or from the main station of Dortmund.

The first time we arrived at the *Hauptbahnhof*, we faced a horrible spectacle. The roof of the main hall had caved in, and only parts of the rafters remained. The floor was covered with rubble. At the entrance of the station, there was a human foot, cut at mid-calf. Strangely, this foot remained there for several weeks! After the initial shock and a few days later, we started to kick this foot from one side to another every time we passed by.

On the evening of October 6, the Dortmund main station was full of passenger trains, and there were many people in these trains or on the platforms—certainly several hundred. Because the bombs fell before the air raid sirens went off, it was carnage. In an underground passage, several corpses were piled up one on top of another. In what had been a waiting room, the floor was covered with a layer of ashes on top of which lay about fifty helmets and gas masks. It was all that was left of the soldiers who were there when incendiary and phosphorous bombs surprised them. In the ripped-open railway cars, there were hundreds of corpses, some of which were atrociously mutilated. I remember having seen the body of a soldier sitting with his hand on his dagger in a passenger car of which only the metal frame was left. He must have been completely charred. Right in the middle of the station, in a locomotive cut in half, was the body of the engineer lying on the window ledge of the cab.

As usual in such circumstances, I wandered here and there, shovel and pick on my shoulder, pretending to be doing something. With my friend André Geerts, I decided to pretend more realistically to be working. We were told that a platform, damaged by a bomb, needed to be cleaned up. We thus went there and started to use our picks and shovels, rather slowly I must say, when suddenly I felt myself lifted up by some strong hands. On that platform, I found myself nose to nose with an SS man who was with two other men in striped clothing.[2] I was made to understand that I was using my pick right on top of an unexploded bomb that these men had come to defuse, which they did a few minutes later. Unbelievably, an SS man had just saved my life! Strangely, as is usual in such a case, I did not feel any fear afterwards. Perhaps it was because, in such an atmosphere, I was no longer my normal self. That same day, my team was used to take down a thirty-meter rail that, all bent, had found itself stuck in the roof of a platform. We were overseen by Herr Schwartz, the firm manager to whom I had earlier said "merde." He recognized me, and, because I did not exert myself very much with this work, he kicked me in the butt. I think he probably took that as a sort of revenge. That was the last time that I saw Schwartz. He was replaced by a man named Schirah.

We worked for a long time in the station. With us, there were some Russians and some Italians, prisoners from the Badoglio army. As I mentioned earlier, they had the letters IMI painted on the back of their jackets. It was rather funny because, at that time, IMI was the trademark of a laundry detergent that was well known in Germany. There were also men in striped clothing from a concentration camp. SS men would bring them every morning and would drive them by beating them with their belts. Looking at that, I would be seized by a feeling of rage and the desire to kill, but I felt powerless. One day when I was not working in the station, my friends related to me that they had witnessed a scene that horrified them. An employee of the Reichsbahn told one of the SS that one of his charges was warming himself at a fire lit between the tracks. This SS coldly killed the poor man with a shot from his rifle. My friends were really upset and revolted by that act, but were unable to intervene since what happened was so fast and unexpected.

—✴— At the *Hauptbahnhof*, one of our first tasks was to clean up the underground passage once the victims' bodies were taken away. We had to break up chunks of concrete with sledge hammers. Sometimes, as I picked up rubble, I found in my shovel pieces of human flesh: an arm or a leg, and once even a torso. Our work there as elsewhere was always accompanied by the yelling of our guards. Often, German civilians who passed near our work sites gave us signs with their fists, as if they wanted us to revolt. In general, they considered the Todt Organization as a sort of penal colony. They were right of course, and we had the proof. Being placed with Todt served as punishment, as was the case for a young Frenchman who was employed by a factory called Union. He came to join us on our work site with one of his superiors. For some infraction, his punishment was a day of work with the Todt. I remember that he found the work very hard and asked us how we managed to keep on going. At the first alert, he disappeared.

As long as we worked at the *Hauptbahnhof*, we would go to a shelter that was located across the street from the station when an alert was sounded. It was quite deep underground. In fact, it was the beginning of a project for a subway. The first part of that underground passage had its vaulted ceiling fairly high and must have been meant for a station. One day that I was in it, a bomb fell right above it. I had the impression that the walls were bending as if they were elastic. The ground seemed to give way under my feet and my ears creaked. Every time we were going to that shelter, we would follow a trail traced in the rubble of the station. Near that trail, as I mentioned earlier, there was that human foot that we kicked thoughtlessly every time we passed by it.

In the days following the bombing, special teams composed of Italian prisoners would pick up corpses and put them on pieces of sheet metal, which served as stretchers. Then they would pile them up in trucks. I remember seeing a man whose head was split in two from the top. It was awful! But there were so many corpses that, in the end, we became indifferent to the spectacle. It is sad to say, but we became accustomed to the horror. Every morning when we arrived at the station, some of my friends who smoked started their workday by going through the railway passenger cars that had arrived to empty the ashtrays. The harvest of cigarette butts was often not very large, so they resorted to looking into the street gutters.

After having cleaned up the rubble and filled in the bomb craters, we were put to work to fix the tracks. Once more, that meant laying ballast and rail ties, installing rails, and securing the ties. As always, we did all this as slowly and as badly as we could, making sure we were not caught. And the first evening of the reopening of traffic, as if by chance, two trains collided. Two people were killed. Our friend Casanova, who was in one of the trains, came out all right. He came back to our camp late that night completely beside himself. He had walked back following the tracks, and he was in shock. Because of this accident, there was a delay of one or two days before the tracks were put back into service. And during this month of October 1944, trains full of refugees coming from the west began to be more numerous. We rejoiced over the panic of these Germans. As far as I was concerned, having lived through my family's evacuation in 1940, I looked upon what was happening as a just return.

Often after a bombing, we would find unexploded incendiary sticks. These things were not dangerous and we could handle them without risk. One time, a friend in my team, Raoul Angot, who moved sand in a wheelbarrow, in his comings and goings was passing by one of these sticks. Every time he passed by it, he would pick it up and would let it fall on its firing pin. After some unsuccessful attempts, all of a sudden flames spurted out, and a liquid fire spread out on the asphalt of the platform that began to burn. Surprised, my friend Raoul panicked and started to throw sand to put out this mini fire. Obviously, he was bawled out by the overseer of the work site. However, things ended well, and we had a good laugh.

Every evening after work, we would go to the station of Dortmund-South to take our special train for Hagen. As it left after a passenger train that had the same destination and was along the same platform, those who arrived early took that train to be first in line for the soup. After a few days, more and more of us were taking that train. Thus, one evening, there was an attempt to keep us from doing so. We were not ready to listen! The light man stopped the train and made us go to the other side of the platform toward our "special" train. However, as soon as he blew his whistle, we would dart across the platform, and the train would stop again. One evening, we made the train stop six times! Later, during the winter, several times, the others and I would hide behind the switching tower at the end of the platform, and jump on the train as it was moving. This meant that we made the trip on the buffers between two cars, and it was really cold!

On Saturday, November 4, 1944, as we were about to have a rest on Sunday, the war decided otherwise. That evening, Allied planes bombed Bochum the same way they had bombed Dortmund on October 6. Since Bochum was further away from my camp than Dortmund, the spectacle was less impressive. However, my work team was organized as a mobile crew and could be sent anywhere, and thus the next day we were at work in the Bochum railroad station. As in the case of Dortmund, we got to it on foot through the ruins of the city as the railroad tracks were cut. It was the same spectacle of chaos, fires, and death, and always there was that odor of blood mixed with that of smoke. The railroad station of Bochum was smaller than that of Dortmund. We did not find as many corpses, but the destruction was the same. Our first job was to clear the destroyed tracks. On the first day, there was the usual confusion following a bombing. As always, we tried to add to that confusion by pretending to be working. We would go from one end of the work site to the other to look at the damage. It is this way that I learned from some fellows that firemen had come down from an apartment building with a woman and her baby in her arms, both dead. My friends were quite upset about that.

In the evening of that same day, we were put to work on a bridge that spanned an avenue. From where we were, we could see a wall of bricks, which was all that was left of a four-story apartment building. There was a strong wind that evening. It fanned the flames of the fires and made the brick wall oscillate. Every time people passed by that wall, our overseers would yell to them to get away. Most would do so, but two men, who probably were going home, did not take the warning seriously. When they saw the danger, however, they began to run, but the wall came crashing down on top of them. They were killed by the bricks.

That night, I do not think that any transport had been planned to bring us back to our camp. Consequently, we had to walk the three miles on railroad ties to reach the marshaling yard of Bochum-Langendreer. With our wooden-soled shoes, this was a pain! Behind us, the fires that ravaged the city lit the sky with a sinister light, which made me shiver. When we arrived in that yard, we found a train full of people who were being evacuated. We did not know where the train was going, but we nevertheless climbed aboard. We settled in a compartment, and we tried to learn the destination of the train. However, nobody seemed to know. In a compartment next to ours, two men, one of whom must have been a musician, were talking. I understood that they were talking about Paris. One of them asked the other in French: "Parlez-vous français?" The answer was "Nein!" At one point, Casanova, who was with us, made this remark aloud: "They don't even know where they are going!" That brought an exclamation in French: "We know it better than you, idiot!" Finally, we realized that the train was going to Hagen where we arrived under an air-raid alert. Since the train stopped in the marshaling yard, we left it and ran to our camp in fear of finding ourselves under bombs.

The following days, before the tracks were repaired, we had to walk several miles to reach our work site. Of course, we delayed getting back to work by dawdling around and straying from the direct path. One day, some of my comrades found themselves in a place where a popular soup was distributed. Being foreigners, they did not have a right to it. However, they had the luck to be seen by some charitable miners who called them and loaned them their helmets. Under this disguise, my friends received a cup of soup. This was a nice gesture of labor fraternity! Unfortunately for me, I was not in the right place that day.

In November, it started to get cold. To warm up during our noon break, we would build a fire along the railroad tracks. Our overseers did not stop us because they could also warm themselves. Since we were not eating, we would gather incendiary sticks and throw them in the fire. It was like fireworks! Once, one of these sticks did not explode as it was thrown in the fire. However, as we had turned our backs to the fire to warm them up, all of a sudden, a boom surprised us. As an instinctive reaction, we all hit the ground. Fortunately, these incendiary sticks did not throw off splinters, only extremely hot flames. On that work site, we were given the job of fixing the ballast and positioning the ties and rails. The latter were thirty meters long. We would carry them with special large pliers. Twelve men were needed to lift one of these rails. Despite the number of men involved, it was very hard work. When the tracks were assembled, we were to secure the ties, but, since we did it so badly, the *Reichsbahn* had the job redone by Russian or Ukrainian women.

Near the end of November, we returned to the *Hauptbahnhof* of Dortmund. There, we took up again the reconstruction of buildings. My work consisted of passing cement blocks to masons. Most of the time, I would take one from a pile, put half of it on my shoulder, the other half resting on the pile, and would wait to move until an overseer or a mason was in sight. This was my way, among others, to slow down the Nazi machine. Now, our days were more and more disturbed by air-raid alerts. That gave us some rest. However, it started to get much colder. Since my clothes were extremely ragged, they did not keep me warm, and I was basically frozen all the time. One morning, as I was starting work, I felt a hand on my shoulder. I turned around and found myself face to face with a German soldier with his combat pack on his back. It was Willi, the employee of the *Telegraphenamt* of Hagen with whom I had often worked. He showed clearly his happiness in seeing me again in the same way one meets an old buddy after a long time. Despite everything that divided us, I could not help to demonstrate the friendship I had for him personally. We spoke for quite a while. He told me that he had been in Holland. At that moment, the overseer of the work site arrived, seemingly angry. He began to holler. However, seeing Willi and me amicably conversing, he was flabbergasted and simply waited till we were finished. I was happy to see Willi again, but that was the last time that we met.

CHAPTER 13

The Ruhr under the Bombs

As I said before, while I was assigned to work at the *Hauptbahnhof* of Dortmund and the Bochum railroad station, I was still housed at the Boeler Heide camp. Overall, I spent a little over eight months in that camp until it was destroyed by the bombing I am about to relate. I was still with the group of buddies that I described earlier. Our lives were regulated by our movements from one work site to another, work, soup, and sleep. And, of course, there was, starting in October, a great increase in the number of Allied air raids on the Ruhr region, the most industrialized section of Germany. Soon, we found ourselves daily under air-raid alerts that started almost always at the same time of the day. During the whole length of each alert, the sky was swept by the beams of hundreds of spotlights, and all the anti-aircraft artillery, composed of hundreds of pieces of all calibers, shot up in the air with a terrific noise. Even if the bombs were not falling on us, we had to seek shelter to avoid shrapnel from the anti-aircraft shells that came back down to the ground. These made a sort of undulating whistling sound that filled the air during the whole time of a raid, which usually lasted a good hour. Besides the bombing of strategic targets such as factories, railroads, bridges, and so forth, the Allies carried out what the Germans called terror-ist bombings. They would spray a city with a rain of explosive ord-nance, incendiary sticks, and phosphorous. Practically all of the region's cities and towns suffered such attacks, one after another, and it was we who were assigned to clear up the debris and make repairs, we the slaves of the Todt. This was the reason why I had been temporarily lent to the *Telegraphenamt* of Hagen.

The Allied plan was to launch a series of air attacks over the Ruhr region, and on December 2, 1944, Hagen was the target. Around eight thirty in the evening, during the distribution of soup, sirens announced a pre-alert by going off three times in a row. Shortly after that, the all-clear was given. As usual, after having eaten my soup, I went to the wash basin to clean myself and my tin. I was back in the barrack when a Belgian fellow, who had gotten some extra soup, came in and offered some. Since I was next to the door, I held out my tin. After having eaten that extra portion, I was about to get back to the wash basin to clean the tin again. As a matter of principle, I made it a point to keep it clean on my shelf. Was it a premonition? Whatever it was, I decided not to do it. Then, a fellow came in, saying that planes were making circles above the town. To reassure myself I went out to see if our camouflage was good, and I thought it was. As soon as I came back to the barrack, the whistling of a bomb made me go out again in a hurry and run to the trench shelter. I saw the red flares that were coming down above the town. It was the signal for the dropping of bombs. I dove into the trench flat on my belly on top of cabbages that were stored there. My roommates followed me as the first bombs fell on our camp, and a blasting mine wiped out the wash basin where I should have been! We felt the wind of the blasts in our trench. I remember having prayed aloud, imploring God to protect us and the Virgin Mary to pray for us. When the raid ended, we heard the last planes fly away. We came out of our shelter to discover our camp totally devastated. A whole row of barracks was burning. Mine was in shambles and was beginning to burn, but my comrades and I arrived on time to extinguish the flames. Approaching my cot, I felt that I was stepping on something. It was my *Jocist* Missal, and it was opened at a page that had an image of a grape harvest scene from the

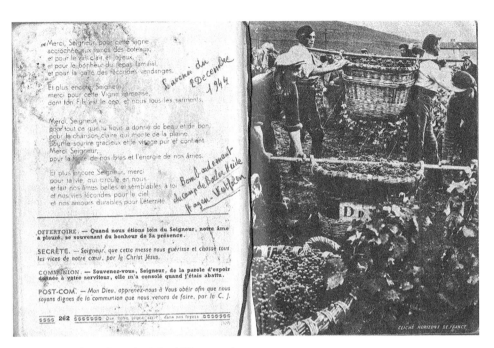

Pages from the *Jociste* Missal Elie stepped on.

Champagne country. Looking at that picture, I noticed that it was a view of my home town, Mareuil-sur-Aÿ! I even recognized some people in that picture. My home, so far! But that evening, I could hope that I would see it again. God had given me a sign!

Considering the state of our dormitories, we were directed to the canteen of a neighboring factory to spend the rest of the night. There, we slept resting on our elbows on the tables. It is during this walk to the canteen that a buddy, Charles Fillioux, made this remark to me: "My old buddy Elie, it's in moments like this that we remember having taken our first communion!" Normally, this fellow played the emancipated man. However, the breath of death had awakened the faith that was dormant within him. And it was in me that he confided, for he saw me making the sign of the cross mornings and evenings. I felt a certain pride and joy in seeing that my testimony and that of my *Jocist* comrades, were bearing fruit. I firmly believed that God had gratified us with His grace so that we could make our faith shine in such circumstances, despite our fear and weakness. During that night, dead tired, I slept on my elbows on a table. At one point, some buddies woke me up to tell me that planes were still circling above us. I answered with a calm that still stupefies me: "Forget it; it's nothing. Sleep!" And they went back to sleep as if I had removed the danger.

The next morning, we were able to see the extent of the disaster. Several barracks were completely destroyed by fire. Where some still stood, we could see several bodies of our comrades like charred tree trunks, most of them Flemish, burned alive in their dormitories. In all, there were seventeen dead and a French fellow seriously wounded. It could have been worse, for a bomb had fallen between two barracks of French workers, but had not exploded. In front of this spectacle, we were gripped by a sentiment of horror, and, without daring to confess it, by a great anguish in imagining what might be in store for us. Our future looked bleak. We felt the shadow of death hover above our heads.

Besides the destroyed barracks, the rest of the camp was in total shambles. There was a big crater right in the middle as well as others throughout the camp. The barracks that were not destroyed were all broken up. Our overseers attempted to make us repair them, but we gave it so little enthusiasm that the work dragged on. Our attitude had the result of exasperating the infamous Jan, who could not help but exclaim: "These young guys screw up everything." That evening, with some workmates, I went to Hagen to spend the night in a bomb shelter. We entered a subterranean passage under a church whose bell had remained suspended half way up the steeple after a recent bombing. After the latest bombing, it had crashed to the ground and lay among ruins. Inside the subterranean passage there was a great number of people still in shock. Many were crying. The place was damp. It was quite chaotic in there, and the atmosphere was so depressing that we decided to return to the camp. To get back to it, we took a trail along and overhanging the railroad tracks. The night was very dark, and a light but penetrating rain was falling. The trail was pockmarked by bomb craters, and one of them that was in front of a house that had been nearly destroyed blocked our way. On the ruins of this house a Nazi flag fluttered. The snaps in the wind of that flag had something sinister about it. We passed under a barbed-wire fence to continue our way. Finally, we spent the night on the floor of the mess hall. Considering the few times we ate in it, this mess hall had never served so much. In the end, the thought of reconstructing the camp was abandoned. The next day, we were transferred to the camp of Hengsteysee. And it is then that I was finally separated from my personal enemy, Jan!

CHAPTER 14

On the Ruhr
Hengsteysee and Herdecke

Hengsteysee was a camp on the bank of the Ruhr River, next to the Hagen-Dortmund road and a six-hundred-yard long bridge that spanned it. At this location and over several miles, the Ruhr formed a sort of lake because of a dam at Wetter. Behind our barracks was an important railroad line that passed through a marshaling yard. A big railroad bridge also crossed the river. On the other side of the road, near the entrance of the camp, a battery of anti-aircraft canons was installed. Our arrival at that camp was unexpected, and we thus spent the night on straw spread on the ground. After several days, we were given a room in one of the barracks. It was December, and it was cold, but we did not have any heat. Thus, we were given two blankets each. I had gotten two good ones, brand new. However, someone stole them when I took them out to air. I was furious. I was able to find two others, old ones, probably those of the thief. Furthermore, for a long time, we did not have any more socks. Every morning, we would wrap our feet with rags, which we called "Russian socks." Of course, at the time to wrap up our feet, these rags were always wet and icy. To add to the picture of this camp, we were invaded by rats. One guy managed to get a hold of some traps, and one evening we were able to kill fourteen!

Because air raids on the Ruhr region had become more and more frequent, Albert Speer, the head of the Todt Organization, started an operation called Ruhr Hilfe, or Aid to the Ruhr. Within the framework of this operation, workers from other regions of Germany, especially from the Sudetenland, were assigned to our camp. These men were not accustomed to the life we led, whether at work or in the camp. They had not yet known bombings. Those who arrived at our camp on December 2 got their baptism by fire. Their deception was great, but they were obliged to share our fate. One day, while we were working in Dortmund, a bomb fell on our latrines and killed an unfortunate Dutch fellow who was using them. The next morning, when we arrived at the Dortmund railroad station, we noticed that the latrines of the work site had suffered the same fate. That led to a joke: "These were the targets of the RAF last night!"

Because Dortmund was repeatedly bombed, my workmates and I were sent there to rebuild an engine depot in the neighborhood of the harbor. We did some masonry and installed metal trusses. The cold was so intense that our hands would stick to the iron. Every time we had to lift an element for the roof onto the walls, those who were on the ground would lose a great amount of time with useless manipulations of that element. And, in all our back and forth, as soon as no overseer was around, we would sneak to a steam engine tender and steal a piece of coal to use in our barrack's stove in the evening. Unfortunately, it was not possible to do that every day.

To get to this work site from our camp at Hengsteysee, we had to get up at five in the morning in the arctic cold of the barrack. As I have explained already, we wrapped up our feet with still frozen rags and put on our clogs with wooden soles. Then, we walked two and a half miles in the snow to get to the small railroad station on the bank of the river opposite our camp. There we boarded a special train. Of course, the train was not heated, and I remember that, if we leaned against the wall of the car, our clothes would stick to it. It is thus that my old trench coat became useless. When I could get a seat, I would sleep the entire trip. After the train had stopped at its destination, we still had to walk another two and a half miles to the work site. One day, several of us, including an overseer, missed the special train. Thus, we took a passenger train later that morning. During our trip, there were several air alerts that forced the train to stop. The last stop was in the countryside before Dortmund. We could hear the bombers arrive. Some of my comrades wanted to get away from the train, but the snow was so deep they could not run. Feeling the blast from the explosion of the bombs, they came back to the train. We were in fact close to Kirchhörde, where there were important factories. We finally arrived at our work site around four in the afternoon. We were rudely received, but those who had arrived on time had not done much during the day because of the alerts.

We spent the months of December 1944 and January 1945 in the Hengsteysee camp. Those were very hard months because that winter was severe, with temperatures reaching ten degrees Fahrenheit. Furthermore, we did not have any shelter to protect us from bombs. Thus, when there was an air alert, and if we had time, we would cross the bridge over the Ruhr. We then climbed a rather steep hill to seek refuge in a cavern that we had discovered in the forest that covered the hill. I went in it once or twice, but I did not feel safe there, and then it gave me claustrophobia. Finally, I preferred to stay at the entrance or to lie on the ground if there was no snow. I would also place myself under the roof of a garden shed to avoid the shrapnel of the flak shells that came back down. It was during one of these nights that, for the first time, I heard a jet plane. After the passage of formations of B-29s above me, I felt a puff of wind like that of a bomb, and I saw in the sky a sort of light that moved. It was probably the exhaust of the jet. I found it strange that a plane had its lights on during a raid. It was much later that I understood what I had seen and heard. It must have been one of the very first German jet fighters. I already had an idea about this type of propulsion, because for several months I had seen the launch of V1 and V2 rockets from ramps that were in the region.

Now, there were at least one or two air alerts every day, and one every evening. Thus, if we had time (and that was not always the case), barely after having eaten our soup, we had to run across the bridge. When there was snow on the ground, it was a real agony. It also happened that we had to wait for the end of an alert before we would be served our soup. Usually, that was because a town of the region was being bombed. One evening, when I gave up the crossing of the bridge, I lay down on the bank of the river. Planes passed over my head and, suddenly, in the distance, I saw luminous dots scintillating in the sky. Those dots got bigger and bigger, forming grapes of fire that transformed themselves into a veritable rain of fire. I realized that it was phosphorous, against which there was no defense. At the end of the raid, I noticed that I had chosen a great spot to lie down indeed—right under a high voltage power line.

During the month of December, we began to feel some strange vibrations in our barracks in the evening, while there was no air raid. We later came to understand that these vibrations were the result of artillery fire. However, these vibrations and the noise of artillery ceased around Christmas, at the time of the German offensive in the Ardennes around Bastogne.

—➤— Hunger pangs plagued us more and more, and food was our main preoccupation. At that time, there was a shortage of salt in Germany. In exchange for cigarettes, my friend in Hagen, who was still working in the central Todt kitchen, gave me some. That salt gave me the opportunity to acquire a few potatoes. Of course, I shared them with my roommates and with some fellows who worked in the kitchen of the camp. Once more, I was robbed. The little salt I had left disappeared.

On Christmas Eve, we stayed up until midnight since we exceptionally did not have to work the next day. At that hour, we all sang together "Minuit Chrétien," "Midnight, Christians." That was an unforgettable moment. In our misery, we felt close to Jesus. With this song, we wanted to affirm our faith and put ourselves in the hands of the Father. We knew that still more dangerous times were waiting for us and that we would suffer even more hunger. Furthermore, we were uncertain about the fate the Nazis reserved for us. On Christmas Day, the weather was as cold as that of the Arctic. André Geerts and I went to the church of Vorhalle to partake in a clandestine mass. We found ourselves among other young men from different camps of the region and a few "transformed" prisoners of war. Altogether we did not form a very large group. The mass was celebrated by Father Louis Gall, a professor of philosophy at the seminary of Soissons. He was one of the priests who had been sent to Germany by Bishop Rodhain to exercise their ministry among us all. As this was forbidden by the Nazi authorities, these priests ministered clandestinely. That morning, we found Father Gall on the church square. He confessed us on the sidewalk. I remember his words after having given his absolution: "Go in peace." But he added: "Be wary of the children!" Indeed, children were playing on the sidewalk, and we could not trust them because they were encouraged to inform on people.

After confession, we entered the church one by one. In his homily, Father Gall made us understand that dangerous and very hard times were waiting for us. He added that we should be prepared to offer our lives for our compatriots, for our country, and for peace. He exhorted us to follow the will of the Lord. Then he made us understand what he risked by his actions, and what the German priests risked by opening their churches to us. On this score, he evoked the concentration camps. But we could not imagine such horrors. To the freezing cold in the church was added the ambiance of tragedy and fear to be called to the ultimate sacrifice. However, this mass revived in us hope as we abandoned ourselves to the grace of God. After the mass, on the recommendation of Father Gall, we left as we had entered, one by one.

During that winter, we had other occasions to see Father Louis Gall because he regularly visited camps while hiding from the Gestapo. Personally, it was only after the war that I truly realized the risks we ran because of our *Jocist* action. Some *Jocists* were arrested and died in concentration camps. One of them, Marcel Callo, was beatified by the Holy Father John Paul II on October 14, 1987. About fifty others suffered the same fate and are now about to be beatified.

In February 1945, we left the Hengsteysee camp for another a few miles away in Erdecke, a small spa. This camp was also on the left bank of the Ruhr River, at the bottom of a wooded hill, next to an important railroad viaduct, fifty meters high. At this location, we were still on the bank of the same lake formed by the dike at Wetter. On the opposite bank there was an electric power plant. Behind us, on the other side of the hill, were the marshaling yards of Vorhalle, a suburb of Hagen. We were thus surrounded by built-up areas, plants, railroad marshaling yards, and strategic arteries, an industrial region called by the Germans Ruhrgebiet. We were thus right in the middle of important targets for the Allied bombers! It was actually my most unfortunate situation since my arrival in Hagen.

Herdecke was to be my last camp before my liberation. The barracks were the same as those of the other camps. The sanitary installations were no better, although we had showers with cold water in a hut with lattice walls. And, besides lice and fleas, there were other bugs. Despite all the means we used to get rid of this scourge, our efforts were in vain. That increased our degeneration. I was again in a barrack with the same buddies. Our group had remained practically the same since the Boeler Heide camp. In our barrack, we met some fellows who were already there. These men were working for a company that was building a bunker as a shelter for the region's *Gauleiter*,[1] in the hill on the right bank of the river. I don't remember them all, but one of them was named Jean Fonse. It seems incredible that his parents had given him that first name, but these were his real first and last names.[2] There was also a strange fellow, who looked like a lawyer's clerk, a maniacal old bachelor, who loudly proclaimed: "If I come back alive, I will proselytize!" It must be said that, since the beginning of January 1945, the whole region was harassed by air attacks: bombings at night by Flying Fortresses and attacks by day by Mosquitos and planes with two fuselages. As did my "lawyer," many other fellows from my barrack promised to go to mass every Sunday if they went home safe and sound.

In my barrack, there was also a fellow who worked in the kitchen of the camp, but I never benefited from the privileged position he held. I remember that his first name was Narcisse. He was part of a small group that was already in the camp before my arrival. Although he was not very exposed where he worked, he had a panicky fear of diving planes that bombed and strafed all over. One day, near the end of March, he took to the roads with the lines of people being evacuated. It must be said that, by then, Germany was experiencing the same debacle that my country had known in 1940. I believe that, in fact, he was not the only one to leave the camp just before Good Friday 1945, the day that marked our encirclement by the Allies. In my case, I preferred to stay put because I feared to find myself in a worse situation if the German army continued to resist for some time. I thought that we would not have long to wait for our liberation. Thus, it was better to stay put. The wait was longer than I had hoped, for our encirclement lasted two weeks.

CHAPTER 15

In Railroad Yards
Still and Again

After nearly two years of slavery, extreme fatigue caused by the hard labor imposed on us, and too little food, we had turned into harassed, famished, and ragged automatons. Our sole aims were to eat and to sleep. We lived like animals. Personally, I needed all the help of my faith to still have some human reflexes. But what lassitude! All of us were desperately waiting for the end of this nightmare.

Around Christmas 1944, we were sent to work in another engine depot, east of Dortmund. It is there that we learned about the battle of Bastogne. Our overseers were proud to tell us that the Americans were retreating. That lowered our morale because we thought that our liberation would be postponed. But we feigned incredulity to defy our oppressors, and we kept the hope that the Allies would win the battle and move onward again.

Thus, I spent the months of January and February on the work sites of the *Hauptbahnhof* and of the engine depots of Dortmund. During all that time, more or less partial bombing raids on the city and its surroundings occurred nearly every day. Often, as we walked to work, we would come across corpses along the railroad tracks. But that had become banal to us. Then, during February 1945, we were given the job to make concrete at the *Hauptbahnhof*. Since diesel was unavailable, we made it using shovels rather than with a mixer. We had to get water in an underground passage that was under construction behind the station. As always, we took our time. One day, as I was outside at the top of the stairs of that passage, I saw a soldier come out of the station, running with his pistol in his right hand. He stopped to ask something of a Serb prisoner who was operating a winch. The latter pointed in the direction of the ruins. The German soldier resumed his running and, soon after, I heard two gun shots. Then the soldier came back slowly, placidly putting his pistol back in its holster. I did not know whom he had shot. However, a woman, passing by trembling with terror, told me: "Did you see? They killed a man! When are we going to be rid of *diese Bande*?" I learned later that the man killed was a prisoner in striped clothing who had taken a civilian coat to flee. He had crouched in the corner of a wall in the ruins, and it is there that he died. I can still see the horrified expression on the face of the Serb prisoner who certainly had not thought of such a denouement.

✈ To fool the German radars, the Allies would drop from the sky some sort of ribbon of various sizes, which had one metallic face and the other painted black. It is thus that, one afternoon, Flying Fortresses surprised the Eckesey neighborhood of Hagen. Since these planes had not been spotted, the alarm sirens had not gone off. The bombs fell on the neighborhood and the railroad marshaling yard when nobody had gone to a shelter. Many people got killed. Following that bombing, my comrades and I were assigned to the job of repairing the tracks. We did not have far to go from our camp to that work site, but we had to walk. Some evenings, it took two of us to help a comrade who was so weak that he could no longer walk.

After another bombing, we remained at this work site. I remember that at the edge of the tracks there was a sugar refinery. It had burned down, but the fire had transformed the sugar into caramel. For us, it was a bit of good fortune! We took as much caramel as we could, but there were so many people who came to do the same that this manna was soon exhausted. During this time, every morning, usually when we arrived on the work site, we were subjected to air attacks. First, formations of Flying Fortresses would bomb neighborhoods and their surroundings. Then we were harassed by the Mosquito fighters that dove onto railway convoys, which were rather numerous in our sector. They bombed and strafed whatever might seem to be a munitions train. All that led to infernal explosions. To get away from the danger, as soon as the first attack began, we would leave the railroad tracks and go as far away as we could. This meant that we would come back only in the evening, just in time to go back to camp. However, as it could have been predicted, these escapades could not last. One morning, as we were about to leave the work site, we were faced by German soldiers with bayonets on their rifles. But our days were no more productive because we spent most of our time on the look-out for planes and seeking refuge under a bridge or in a shelter dug into a berm on the side of the marshaling yard. The Mosquitos that bombed the Vorhalle marshaling yard would dive over our heads, and, when we were under the bridge, we could feel the blast from the bombs.

One afternoon, I had taken refuge under a railroad car when a Mosquito, as it was ending its dive, let go of a napalm bomb. It fell on the tracks about fifty yards from me. I saw a sheet of fire cover the ground. When the fire had died down, I saw a bunch of guys, who had lain down in the hollow of the ballast between tracks, get up and run to the shelter. They were somewhat singed but none lost his life! I also came out from underneath the car and began to run in the direction of the shelter. However, a Todt overseer, who had also taken refuge under the same railroad car as I did, began to yell: "Nicht rennen!" "Don't run!" Then, he emphasized his order by hitting me on the back with his fist. Just a few days before, an SS man, who was overseeing another part of the work site, had coldly shot and killed a Polish fellow because he thought that the latter had gotten back to work much too late after an air attack. Given this barbarity, we had to expect the worst.

On a February night I was awakened by the explosion of bombs that were falling nearby. I was dead tired, and my sleep must have been very deep, for I had not heard the sirens. When I went out of my barrack, I was blinded by flashes on all sides. My camp was not hit, but another, also of the Todt, was totally destroyed. The next day, we welcomed comrades who no longer had a place to sleep. Fortunately, they were all safe and sound.

As I have already said, that winter was very harsh, especially at the beginning of 1945. As the days went by, I felt myself weakening more. Despite my faith, sometimes depression got ahold of me. Hunger, always hunger, an hallucinating pain! I cannot find the words to describe what all of us were going through. I remember that one evening, in the train that brought us back from our work site, I dreamt that a spoon was nearing my mouth. And it was with an opened mouth that I woke up. One afternoon, when I had not gone to work, I dragged myself to a meadow near the marshaling yards of Vorhalle between two Mosquito attacks. I went there to cut dandelions. I wanted to do it fast, but I was without strength. I wanted to run, but my legs would not cooperate. I really had a tough time going back up the hill. After having washed my dandelions, I ate them raw with a little vinegar, and, with the same difficulty, I climbed into my bed. I was incapable of doing anything else while waiting for the time of the soup. I must have looked very bad because, one evening, coming back from the distribution of the soup, a buddy, whose name was Richard and who lived in another barrack, said to me: "You've got a *sale gueule*!"[1] He added: "Narcisse does not give you anything to eat?" He was talking about the cook, who had not left yet, and who had indeed never offered me so much as a crumb of bread. My exhaustion and my state of depression were such that my will was practically annihilated. This weakness did not last. One evening, I had a moment of revolt and could not help from yelling: "I am fed up with being hungry!"

⟶ On March 7, 1945, the day of my twenty-fourth birthday, I spent the whole morning fearing that I would be killed that day. I couldn't say why I felt that way. However, it did almost happen! Indeed, around ten in the morning, a Flying Fortress formation flew in our direction, bombing the marshaling yard of Hengsteysee in passing. As soon as we heard the humming of the planes, we left the railroad tracks. A short while later, I found myself with two comrades near a half-destroyed house. I proposed that we seek shelter in a hole made by a bomb next to it, saying that no two bombs fell in the same place. One of my two friends refused, saying that he preferred to lie down on the ground because that made him laugh! As the planes arrived above us and began to drop bombs, we quickly hit the ground. At that moment, I felt the blast of a bomb that was stronger than others. Curiously, it produced a draft in my pants' legs. In fact, the impact was very close to us, and the explosion of a five-hundred-pound bomb makes an incredible noise, and it "splatters"! When the smoke dissipated, the same buddy exclaimed to me: "Look at where your house is!" I turned in that direction and saw that the bomb had fallen close to the house and that the house had crumbled into the hole where I wanted to seek shelter.

During this winter of 1944–45, I often escaped death simply because I was not where I should have been. Many of my friends had the same good fortune. For example, my friend Casanova had told us that, in case of a bombing, he would seek shelter inside a rectangular concrete box that was between two railroad tracks. On the morning of March 7, back on the work site after the bombing, we saw the crater of a bomb where that concrete box had sat. For a while, we asked ourselves what had happened to Casanova. Fortunately for him, he had changed his mind at the last moment.

Our work site was located between the neighborhood of Eckesey and the town of Boele, a suburb of Hagen. This was not far from our old Boeler Heide camp. Thus, when the sirens announced an air raid, we would run to it to seek refuge in the dugout that we had used before. The camp no longer existed. However, we all found ourselves in that trench one early March afternoon. As usual, we heard the humming sound that grew louder and louder, and then the noise of thunder was followed by an earthquake. This formation of Flying Fortresses had dropped its bombs on a target in our sector. When the planes went away, we uttered a sigh of relief. However, what we had seen was only one wave of a vast air raid. Again, we heard the humming noise that grew louder, and again the earth shook. This happened several times that day! The last wave of planes dropped its bombs above us. Some bombs fell on the railroad tracks but many more fell on houses nearby.

On March 12, around four in the afternoon, sirens wailed once more *Vollalarm*. And once more, my friends and I found ourselves in our trench shelter. The planes passed over us, flying toward Dortmund. What happened next was like a ravaging cyclone. Over a thousand bombers and fighters unloaded their one- and two-ton bombs on ruins. In our shelter the earth trembled, and we were terrified even though we were not directly under this deluge. I believe that the whole thing lasted around three-quarters of an hour in a single wave. It was hell! Soon afterward we learned the scope of this air raid from prisoners who had a radio.

One Sunday, instead of going to work, I went to town with two packs of cigarettes, one of which belonged to a roommate. I intended to exchange them for bread with my cook friend who worked in the central Todt kitchen. I was not sure it would happen, but it did. I left to return to my camp with two bread balls in my bag. When I arrived at the street that overlooked the marshaling yard where everyone worked, I noticed two S.A. men in uniform. I hesitated for a moment. Then, taking hold of myself, I walked toward them. Of course, they stopped me and asked why I was not working. Then the Holy Spirit inspired me. I told them that I was employed by the firm that was building a bunker in Wetter for the *Gauleiter* of the region, that is, on the other bank of the Ruhr River. In fact, in my barrack, there was a team of workers assigned to the Firma Buntzer, which was building that bunker. The two S.A. men patted me down. Seeing the two balls of bread, they asked me what it was. I told them that it was the food ration for the Buntzer team. After talking with each other, these two let me go. I must say that I got a real fright, but I left them without waiting to hear more!

One day during March, when my friends and I were loading railroad cars with cement in a Todt depot at Hengsteysee, our overseers promised us that we would be able to go back to our barrack as soon as the work was done. Since at this juncture the pace of our work no longer had much importance, after this promise we made a real effort to get the job done fast. Our overseers, however, changed their minds and began to talk about our going to Dortmund with these railroad cars. After considering the state of the tracks and the strafing of Allied planes, we were sure there was a chance we would never arrive at that destination. Thus, to show our refusal, we stopped working. We had barely stopped when the depot's SS guard and his German Shepherd arrived. He threatened us with his machine gun. Thus, we got back to work, but at an extremely slow pace, with always a good part of the team in the latrines, so that the loading lasted until the end of the day. The decision to go to Dortmund was abandoned. I believe that this train never left the depot and was still there at the end of the war.

—✈— As I said before, we remained at work in the marshaling yard of Hagen the whole month of March and until our liberation. During the night of March 16, Hagen was bombed again, this time more thoroughly than before. Again there were destruction and death. A huge bomb crashed headlong into the side of a multi-story bunker, leaving an enormous hole in its wall. Later, my friend the cook, who had a room on the second floor of Todt *Leitstelle*, related to me that one afternoon, during an air raid, he saw through his window the last bomb of a bomber's load coming right at him. He told me: "I was dumbfounded by the sight, not being able to move, as if I was hypnotized!" Fortunately for him, the bomb fell farther away.

During that month, the disorganization of the Nazi system increased. One day, we found that our military guards had disappeared. From then on, we went to our work site, did practically nothing, and left as we pleased. What was important was to show up to get our food tickets. When sirens started to howl, André Geerts and I would go seek refuge in a quarry on the heights of the town. From there we could see the Mosquitos and the double fuselage planes bombing and strafing everywhere—tracks, flak batteries, and anything that seemed to be a military or industrial target. We had to watch out for shrapnel and lost bullets that fell all around. One evening, as we were returning to our camp, we saw a strange spectacle. Flying Fortresses were passing at a low altitude, one behind another, each dropping one bomb on the marshaling yard. André and I waited until it was over before going across the tracks and getting back to our barrack. Our comrades thought we were dead!

Around that time, during a raid, planes dropped leaflets that had a proclamation from General Eisenhower. The general was advising foreign workers to stay away from railroads. That concerned us of course because it was easier said than done. Our camp was in the middle of railroad junctions and of important factories. The Allies had declared the Ruhr to be a "Zone of Death." Indeed, fighter planes shot at everything that moved. Thus, one afternoon, during an attack from Mosquitos, I found myself alone on a street sloping up toward the town center. I did not have time that day to go to the quarry. I took refuge in an alley, between the wall of a school and a berm covered with bushes. That formed a sort of a trench. A squadron of Mosquitos strafed the street as they dove over the railroad tracks. All of a sudden, I heard a woman's voice yelling: "Die Bandite, die Bandite!" "Bandits! Bandits!" It was a young woman, totally beside herself, who was walking up and down the street risking death. I came out of my refuge, took her by the hand, and brought her to the alley. She told me that a few days before, on March 12 to be exact, she was in Dortmund right at the time of the terrible bombing that we had observed from our trench shelter in our old camp of Boeler Heide. That explained her panic. I do not remember what she looked like. I only remember that she was rather young. I could not say whether I had found her pretty. In such moments of fear, only survival was important.

During our wandering around, André Geerts and I would meet people who, like us, were trying to find shelter from bombs. One evening, as we were at the entrance of a trench shelter, we distinctly heard a German say: "Why don't we let the Americans come? Are we waiting for the Russians to come?" Already a few weeks before, I had heard an employee of the Strassenbahn openly say that she no longer believed in anything. The Germans were becoming more and more demoralized. Since the beginning of the year, however, we could see young men, some as young as fourteen, and old men in their sixties in dark green uniforms that must have been left over from World War I. These were troops that formed the Volkssturm.[2] Most were armed with an anti-tank grenade called *Panzerfaust*. Their role was to guard roads and to man anti-tank obstacles. In fact, when I was still working at the Dortmund *Hauptbahnhof*, I did see a poster proclaiming the raising of this "army." The poster was signed by Himmler. Once, as I worked close by, a German called to me, pointing to the poster, and said: "They are now mobilizing boys and old men, and it is signed Himmler. He is worse than Hitler! Besides, Hitler died on July 20!" He was making reference to the assassination attempt that took place on July 20, 1944. However, Hitler was only wounded. But, already many Germans thought that he was indeed dead.

At the end of March, those who ordered us around were completely confused. They no longer knew how to organize work. And of course we added to the chaos. It came to the point that our masters tried to make us work at night on the tracks. However, since there was no other light than that of the moon, we simply leaned on our shovels. From afar, we would marvel at the flashes of the battle. From time to time, it looked like fireworks. All this was the fire of a tragedy that was coming to an end. But many more people would die before the final act.

At the time of Holy Week, the encirclement of the Ruhr was about to be realized. We were suffering, but the hope of our liberation was growing. One night, while coming back from the latrines, a buddy from Gascony told us with the beautiful accent of his home: "I believe that tanks are arriving. I have heard a clanking noise!" Obviously, we remained skeptical and rather mocking. However, he was right. But the tanks took their time to reach us. One evening, one of ours did not come back to the barrack. He had been killed by a bomb on the work site. I believe it was Jean Fonse, but I am not sure.

On March 30, Good Friday, we did learn that in fact the Ruhr region was surrounded by Allied forces. Considering our geographical position, we were right at the center of that encirclement. We hoped that this would not last too long, but we feared that the Nazis would resist ferociously. We expected the worst from these fanatics. At any rate, for us, the following days were exhausting because of the increased intensity of the bombings and strafing. This ordeal put our nerves on edge. However, we practically no longer worked, but we still got soup tickets from a friend who had stolen them!

On April 1, Easter Day, I went to mass at the parish church. In the afternoon, Father Louis Gall came to pay us a visit especially to tell us that he was going to celebrate mass in the church of Vorhalle in the evening. I remember that he shared with us some small biscuits with paté that were more than welcomed by us. Every time that Father Gall came to celebrate mass, he would confess us. I never could do it with a German priest, although I would have loved to. As ever, with André Geerts, I thus participated in the celebration of that mass of the Resurrection, once more clandestinely. An immense hope was within us but also the apprehension about what would be our last days of captivity. We were wondering how long that could take. That day, having already taken communion at the parish mass, I did it a second time. Like Jesus at Easter, my comrades and I were feeling close to our resurrection.

CHAPTER 16

My Last Week as a Slave

Monday, April 9, 1945

That day, my comrades and I went to the work site. At the beginning of the afternoon, however, we were sent back to our camp. There, we were all assembled and were told that we had to go to a village on the opposite bank of the river to build defense works. We were ordered to pack our bags because we would be housed there. While we were getting ready, Flying Fortresses passed over us without dropping bombs. Still, we went to seek refuge in our trench shelter. While there we heard explosions followed by whistling noises. This was something we had not yet heard. At first, we thought that it was Mosquitos dropping bombs, but we were mistaken. At any rate, once the alert was over, we took the road to our new work site. We thus crossed the Ruhr River and then we walked about six miles. When we arrived at our destination, we were informed that we could not be housed that night. We were told to return to our camp and to come back the next day.

With some friends, I returned to our camp by taking trails through the countryside. As we passed by a village, we saw broken telephone poles with hanging wires. In the fields there were small, flared, shallow craters. I remarked to my companions that these must be the result of artillery shells. (As it turned out, I was right; as we learned later, American tanks had punched through the German defenses that afternoon.) We thus came back to our camp dead tired. Each of my heels had a blister. I was in great pain.

Tuesday, April 10

Early that morning, trucks arrived in our camp to take us to the place we had gone the day before. Not wanting to dig trenches for our prison guards, I pulled up my covers and stayed in my bunk. Several of my roommates did the same. A little later, a male nurse came to our barrack and, seeing us, asked why we had not gone to work. I tried to tell him that I was sick, but he made me get up as well as the others, and he sent us to the office of a company that was located near a railroad bridge at the lower end of our former Boeler Heide camp. There, on a spur, were several railroad cars full of supplies and food evacuated from Dortmund before the advance of the Americans. We were told to unload these cars and to store the supplies in a barrack on the side of the track. I took advantage of this job to put aside working clothes and two pounds of sugar, as well as other things, including a pair of boots that I gave to a buddy because they did not fit me.

Our overseer was from the Rhineland, from the city of Cologne to be exact. His name was Keller, and he spoke French without an accent. In the afternoon, he asked me to take a Tyrolian backpack full of food to his wife, who lived in the town of Dahl, some eight miles from where we were. To go there, he gave me a bicycle that I was to leave with his wife. He asked me to do this because he knew that I spoke German and thus that I could manage on my own. I climbed on the bicycle and left. I went through Hagen in ruins. It was a spectacle of desolation. What was left of walls looked like skeletons. I had to wind my way around the rubble. Along the way, in what had been an avenue of the city, I saw the bloody imprint of a human body, arms extended, who must have been flung against what was left of a wall by the explosion of a bomb. The sight of this chaos wrung my heart even though, for months now, I had become accustomed to such a spectacle. Nevertheless, I could not feel too sorry, for my buddies and I had waited so long for this moment. These ruins were telling us that our liberation was near. I was still in Hagen when I met young Luxemburgers with whom I had worked at the *Telegraphenamt*. From afar, they waved at me, yelling a loud and happy "Elie" despite the tragic background. In the countryside, along the road, I came across columns of *Volkssturm* men, a *Panzerfaust* on one shoulder, walking like automatons.

Arriving in Dahl, I found Mrs. Keller with several people from the village at the entrance of a cave that served as their shelter. I gave her the bicycle and the bag, and I quickly left, for now I had to walk back to where I had started. By chance, a worker who was driving a small electric truck was going in the same direction as I was. I asked him if I could jump in. He accepted, and I rode with him for about three miles. When I left this man, I still had about six miles to walk. That day I wore a pair of shoes that I had bought from a friend for very cheap. They were tight on me and naturally tore open the blisters on my ankles. These were raw when I got back to the office.

Since it was rather late, my comrades had already returned to the camp. (The next day, I learned that they had to seek refuge from artillery shots several times along their route.) Thus, I found myself alone with the firm's director, a man whose name was Schirah. He was completely beside himself and was packing his bags. He told me that his wife was in a nearby town. He wanted to be with her, but he did not know where the Americans were. I advised him to stay put, but he continued to get ready to go. Then he sent me to another office to pick up certain things. That place was about fifty yards away. On my way, I heard artillery shots. Instinctively, I leaned forward but continued to walk, not thinking about hitting the ground. Fortunately, the shells were falling a lot farther away. Strangely, I was not afraid of the artillery. Perhaps it was because I thought that artillery shots were more precise than the planes' unloading of bombs that had so terrorized us. When Schirah had finished packing, he took me to that second office where there was a small kitchen. There he grilled two cutlets in butter that we ate with a large slice of barley bread. Since I had not seen so much food in months, I ate faster than it takes to speak about it. Then, we went to the other office, which was near a bunker. As we entered the bunker, Schirah told me that, during the night he would give me his pistol because he would send me to check around the barrack where my friends and I had stored what we had unloaded from freight cars. He was afraid that Russians from a nearby camp might go on a looting rampage. Obviously, I was not interested in this proposition, and it was he who went out to check around.

Thus, I spent the night in that bunker with some people from the neighborhood. Men who had fought in World War I were reminiscing. One spoke about shell holes deep enough to swallow a house. In the end, I spent the night sleeping like a baby.

Wednesday, April 11

That morning, as I came out of the bunker, an employee from the office handed me a piece of paper entitling me to a double ration of soup to compensate for the one I had missed the day before! Having nothing else to do in that place, I decided to return to my camp. Feeling the effects of the miles I had covered by foot the day before and my ankles still raw, each step that I took was an ordeal. I shuffled along rather than walked.

On my way, under a railroad bridge, I had to pass through some anti-tank barriers that *Volkssturm* men were guarding. They let me pass, but they were stunned as they saw the direction I was taking. Indeed, I was going straight in the direction of the front. When I arrived on the bank of the Ruhr, I saw that the bridge at the entrance of the town had been blown up. At that point, I took the trail that led to the camp. This trail passed under a railroad viaduct. As I got close to it, I saw a curious spectacle. The viaduct was full of military vehicles and people who followed them. They were fleeing the Americans' advance. The jumping of these vehicles on the railroad ties had a comical effect.

When I arrived at the camp, I saw that the Germans had deployed a battery of artillery behind our barracks. The Americans, who were still several miles away, were shelling all of our sector— that is, railroad tracks, the Vorhalle and Hengsteysee marshaling yards, and German positions in the woods behind our camp. All day long, we heard the whistling of shells passing above our heads. Sitting next to our shelter, we tried to follow them with our eyes. We must have resembled spectators at a tennis match!

That evening, the soup was composed of chickpeas. Since I could get two rations, I was given two full tins. Of course, I thought I could eat it all. However, my stomach had shrunk and couldn't take in such a quantity, especially of this type of pea. And what had to happen happened. The chickpeas began to ferment in my stomach, to the point that I could no longer bend down. At nightfall, a few buddies and I went to seek shelter in a small trench that was a bit outside the camp. Only five or six people could fit in this trench, and I remember that I had a tough time sitting down. When we left for that trench, some comrades yelled at us: "During the day, you watch the shells pass by and, because it is night, you are going to the shelter! Well, we are going to sleep in our pad!" However, these guys did not stay long in their pad. The Americans, who had arrived at the Ruhr River, began to shell even more. The Germans, with their 105 mm cannons, joined the concert. The noise was infernal, especially after a shell fell on the munitions caisson of a German battery at the entrance of the camp. That produced a series of explosions that lasted several long minutes. In this storm, by some miracle, only one horse was killed. In the end, the retreating troops blew up the viaduct.

The chickpeas continued to have their effect. During the night, I had violent stomach pains. I was forced to leave the shelter to relieve myself. As I came out of the trench, I bumped into the body of a friend lying on the ground under a blanket, his head under a stool! It was my friend from Gascony. I asked him if he was not afraid. He answered with his beautiful accent: "I see nothing, I hear nothing, I figure I am in a shelter!" Fortunately for him, no shell fell close by. My diarrhea made me sick all the next day, but finally it stopped relatively quickly.

Thursday, April 12

From this day on, we were in a no-man's land. The artillery shots were rather numerous, but, curiously, I still was not afraid. However,

I kept a certain prudence by staying close to the shelter. We accustomed ourselves to the situation, and we made efforts to discover the positions of the American batteries. According to the place where shells were fired, we could determine what the target was. And the same batteries would always fire on the same targets.

One of our comrades, who was a butcher, cut a few "beef steaks" from the horse killed the previous day. Each of us was able to eat one cooked in oil that the Todt had brought from other camps, now in the hands of the Allies. What a feast it was!

I told my buddies what I had been doing on Tuesday and had indicated where the supplies were stored. In the afternoon, some of them decided to go there to try to take whatever they could. They took the trail along the lake.[1] Since they were in the open, American machine guns fired at them. One of them, Charles Filloux, was wounded in the thigh. I learned later that he was transported to the nearest hospital and was well taken care of. As for me, my belly now in peace, I passed a second night in the trench.

Friday, April 13

That morning, when we came out of the trench, we saw on the ground some sort of metallic cylinders whose ends were serrated. We asked ourselves what these things were. I soon realized that they were pieces of shrapnel from shells that exploded in the air. As we prepared to go to our barrack, hoping to cook another horse steak, we heard one cannon shot, then a second, and a third, and the explosion of a shell near us. We ran into the barrack, but, as shots were fired again, we dove back into the trench that was in the middle of the camp. The shots continued all morning. Thus, we had to forget about our steak. I do not remember what we ate that day or the following days. No doubt, the kitchen operated more or less well. Our Todt overseers were still with us, and they were not about to go hungry!

At one point during the morning, we noticed that there were no longer any shots being fired from the Germans' side. They had obviously retreated. Thus, the afternoon was much calmer. André Geerts, another friend, and I stayed in the woods near our little trench. Around three or four in the afternoon, we heard a cannon shot. From where it was coming, I thought right away that it was for us. And, just as I thought, a shell exploded about fifty yards in front of us. We dove into the trench. The artillery men lengthened their shots and swept the woods at the edge of our camp. When this shooting stopped, we came out of our shelter. In the open, we saw the haversack of one of us, which had been left outside, riddled with shrapnel. But this was the last shot of artillery on our camp.

In the evening, several of us got ready to spend another night in our small shelter. As we were waiting for the night to fall, while sitting next to the entrance, we saw some German soldiers installing a machine gun at the edge of the woods, a few yards from us. It was quite clear that they were passably drunk. The *Feldwebel*[2] who was in command approached. He asked us if we were French. We told him yes. Then he asked if we had any weapons. We reassured him on this score, for how could we have been able to acquire some. In the end, he told us that he trusted us. Then, he added: "At nine o'clock, go into your shelter, for they are coming across with flamethrowers." I asked him: "Why are you still fighting? The war is about over!" He answered: "We are soldiers; we have to do our duty till the end." I must say that we did not take him seriously. In fact, the night was calm. In hindsight, I believe that if the Americans had attacked with flamethrowers, we would not have survived that night.

Saturday, April 14

When we came out of our shelter, we saw that the German soldiers had left, as we had thought they would. They had not fired a shot, and there was an unusual calm. The morning went by without anything troubling that calm. In the afternoon, we saw a small boat cross the Ruhr and dock at the bank below our camp. Two men came up. They were Frenchmen, whose camp was on the other side of the lake, who had already been liberated by the Americans. One of the two told us that his name was De Connings. He had a pistol in his belt and a tricolor roundel on his jacket. He thought that we had also been liberated. I remember how our Todt overseers and the few German soldiers who were still with us were stunned as this man came near them. De Connings offered to an Italian colonel, who was a prisoner of war, to take him across the river. The Italian colonel declined the invitation. De Connings then left, and nobody did anything to keep him or to shoot him.

In the evening, at nightfall, we heard again a cannon shot and a few seconds later an explosion in the bushes on the lake's shore. That first shot was followed by others to clear up the ground on the bank of the Ruhr. Actually, the shots came from mortars. My friends and I amused ourselves by measuring the time between the shots and the explosion of a shell. We calculated fifteen seconds. A buddy, who wanted to retrieve something from his barrack, told us: "I'm going to dash out at the time of a shot and count to fifteen. I should have enough time!" Winded, he came back very quickly saying: "I was already at the count of ten when I was not even half way!" That night, we slept much better than during the previous nights.

Sunday, April 15

I do not remember what happened during the morning, but I have kept an imperishable memory of the hour: three pm! At that precise hour, two GIs, with machine guns, came down the hill and entered our camp.

WE WERE FREE!

Then, there was an explosion of joy. We jumped, we cried, and we laughed at the same time. We expressed at the top of our lungs our joy to find freedom and peace again. Finally, the nightmare was over. We were about to live again, to live as free men. Our joy was immense, and we hoped for the best in the future!

The two GIs brought together our overseers, as they were in uniform. Unfortunately, the important ones had fled, and only the lower ranks were among them. One of these, a Flemish guy who spoke English, argued that they were just workers. The Americans took them into custody nevertheless. As soon as they were gone, we invaded their barracks and looted anything that might be of use for us, such as food and shoes among other things. In my case, I took a big piece of bread and a pint of Cognac (Camus, three stars). To drink to our liberation, I shared the bottle with two buddies. Each of us got a pretty good amount! I drank what I had in one gulp and then went to lie down on my bunk. I thought I was going to be really plastered. Curiously, the cognac did not do me any harm! Later on, our Germans came back and found their barracks looted. They pleaded with us to give them back at least their shoes. But those who had taken them refused. Our guards then left in sweaters and slippers. It was a very sweet little revenge!

CHAPTER 17

Peace and Return to Mareuil-sur-Aÿ

On April 16, 1945, the weather was perfect. The sun shone, and it seemed that spring was giving the nature around us a festive air to fall in with our immense joy. In the afternoon, I went to the lakeshore alone. There, I savored for a few moments this peace finally found again. And I said a prayer of thanksgiving. I thanked God for having permitted me to see this day, safe and sound. On the lake, there were people, probably Americans, who were sailing in small boats. A phonograph was playing music that came all the way to me. How I enjoyed that moment! Everything was calm—no more planes, no more bombs. Still today, I believe that this was one of the most beautiful days of my life. At any rate, it was the day that left the greatest mark on me.

The next day, several buddies and I took to the road intending to return to France by foot. It was perhaps a silly idea, but we were in such a hurry to see our families again! We took with us the most important of our possessions, and we crossed the lake in small boats steered by young Germans. When we docked at Wetter, a town on the opposite bank of the lake, Americans took us into custody. They drove us in a Dodge truck to Dortmund. There, we were confined for three weeks in the city's *caserne*. This *caserne* was immense. It was practically a small town with tree-lined alleys and rather luxurious installations. These, however, had been ransacked by Russians, who were about to be repatriated. There were many of them.

These people were rather unpolished. All day long, they would circulate on bicycles in the alleys of the *caserne*. It seemed that they had never seen a bike in their lives. What was funny were their attempts at back-pedaling. Since all German bicycles were built with a brake on the hub of the rear wheel, pedaling backwards caused the bikes to stop abruptly, and "our" Russians would fall to the ground. Then, they would look all around the bike without understanding what had happened.

The three weeks spent in that *caserne* seemed like an eternity. This was particularly the case because food was not abundant, and we were still hungry! Fortunately, during this forced stay, Father Louis Gall contacted us again. On Friday, April 27, he got us together for a "Holy Hour," which was an unforgettable hour of meditation. On May 1, he celebrated mass for us in a building of the *caserne*. I remember that in his homily he urged us to find again love for work well done after a long time of lazing around and sabotaging whatever we did when it was possible. This advice was not useless because many of us were rather disoriented and surely would have had a hard time adjusting to normal life.

Finally, on the evening of May 8, we were told that we would leave the next morning. Thus, on May 9, we climbed into GMC trucks whose drivers were black men. We ended up in Münster, where we spent the day. In the evening, we were given C rations and then left that city by train. I found myself in a freight car without a roof that had served to transport coal! My comrades and I thought that we would receive some more C rations, for the box we had received had not lasted very long. However, we had nothing more to eat for a good part of the journey. The train crossed the Rhine on a temporary bridge that night. During the morning of May 10, the train passed along the Siegfried Line. I was able to see bunkers ripped apart by bombs. In some of them, there were still some corpses. Along the track, some people came to salute us. Some fellows in my group responded with jeers. I remember that the train stopped somewhere, but not where exactly. There, all of us were subjected to a dusting of DDT, a product that we did not yet know. Then, the train passed through Mönchen-Gladbach and, in the afternoon, it crossed the border of Holland. At that point the Dutch people greeted us, waving little flags. It is only at that moment that I learned of the capitulation of Nazi Germany. That evening, the train stopped in Maastricht where Red Cross volunteers gave all of us some soup. The next stop was Liege, where we arrived around midnight. The city was celebrating with fireworks. Some people gave us white bread, apples, and milk. They were rejoicing. They told us about their past woes, including the bombings by V2s, which they called "robots." They were so welcoming that it reminded me of our passing through Braine-le-Comte as we were going into Germany. The warmth of their friendliness was the same, but obviously this time joy replaced sadness.

The next day, May 11, the train stopped in Namur, where we were given a meal at noon. That evening, we finally arrived in France. We crossed the border near Givet, and our final destination was Charleville-Mézières. As we came out of the train, we were directed to a repatriation center. During the day of May 12, after a medical check-up, we went to an office where we were asked many questions about the circumstances of our deportation and living conditions during our forced labor in Germany. Finally, we were given repatriated identity cards.

At a very early hour on May 13, I took a train that was, finally, going to bring me back home. At that point, I was now separated from those with whom I had lived through so much misery, fear, and physical and moral suffering. I was in a hurry to arrive because, this May 13, was the feast of St. Joan of Arc, the saint liberator of France. Therefore, I wanted absolutely to arrive at Mareuil early enough to be able to attend mass at the village church. When my train arrived in Reims, I was told that the Rilly-la-Montagne tunnel, through which the track to Epernay passed, was destroyed. Taking a direct train to Epernay was impossible. By chance, my train was passing through Châlons-sur-Marne and made a stop there. At the station I was able to climb on board a train of repatriated prisoners that was going in the direction of Paris. This train stopped in Epernay. In the station's courtyard, a welcoming center had been installed

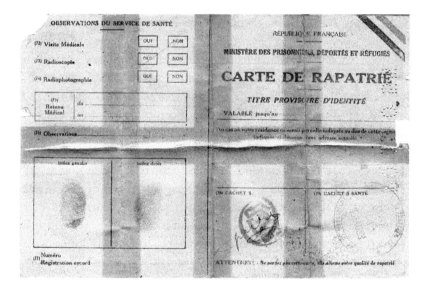

Elie's repatriation card.

under a sort of tent. There, while I was waiting to find some means of transportation to Mareuil-sur-Aÿ, I was served a glass of Champagne. Suddenly, it came to my mind that I had had no news of my family for nearly a year. I went to a young lady, a Mademoiselle Dourdan, who was in charge of the reception desk of the welcoming center. I knew that she was from Mareuil, and, in fact, I knew her well. I asked her about my family. She reassured me in saying: "Be at ease, everybody is doing fine!" I remember to have asked also: "What about my little brother?" She answered that he was doing fine and was still very cute. Then, we spoke for quite a while about events that took place in the Champagne region since my departure.

As it turned out, I did not have to wait too long to get transportation to Mareuil. I had the luck to meet one of my former clients from Louvois, who had come to pick up a prisoner from his village. He invited me as well as a prisoner from Aÿ to climb in his car, and we took off. As we drove through Aÿ, I was able to see the ruins of a neighborhood that had been bombed during the summer of 1944. This was something that I had not known. Finally, we arrived in Mareuil-sur-Aÿ. My former client, whose name I have forgotten, stopped his car in front of my house. It was he who opened the door of the courtyard. Then, he announced to my mother and my little brother Jean, who were on the threshold of the kitchen door: "Would you not want a newspaper seller?" My mother, nonplussed for a few seconds, understood and ran to me to kiss and hug me.

We hugged each other, letting our tears flow, tears of joy! It was a moment of unforgettable happiness, the long-awaited end of a nightmare. My little brother Jean was looking at me. He did not seem to understand what was going on. He had barely known me when he was a baby.

My other brother, Roger, who was now fifteen years old, quickly jumped on his bicycle to bring the good news to my father. As usual on Sundays, he had gone very early, with my youngest sister, Micheline, to work in his vegetable garden located outside of Mareuil, some two miles from where we lived. My mother prepared a bath for me in a large bucket. I washed, and was refreshed and clean. When my father arrived, I hugged him tightly. He had tears in his eyes; tears of joy in seeing me again. Ultimately, my father,

Micheline, Roger, and I went to the church to attend High Mass. I had arrived in time. Once more God had answered my prayers!

That afternoon, my sisters Jeanne and Rolande came from Reims, where they worked. Two American soldiers, Ivan and Lloyd, the first from Illinois and the second from Kansas, had driven them in a jeep. Ivan was engaged to Rolande, and Lloyd was very much in love with Micheline. It is thus that I met my two future brothers-in-law. A few weeks later, I got to meet my third brother-in-law, Alfred Godfroy, who was engaged to Jeanne.

⟶ This is the end of the story of what I went through during this war that afflicted our planet. Is it possible to make others feel deeply, by writing or speaking, the physical and moral sufferings, the work that was too hard, the horrible hunger, the harsh cold, the burning heat on the railroad tracks, the frightful bombings, and especially the humiliation of our condition of being slaves? I don't know. However, while I am not a writer, I want a trace of this testimony of the succession of events and various situations to survive after I have passed on. And I want my family and my descendants to learn from this terrible period of my life.

For me, the names of Dortmund, Bochum, and Hagen still today after some seventy years, evoke in my mind death, ruins, suffering, hunger, anxiety, and especially this fear of the bombings. During that war, millions of other men and women suffered a lot more than I did, often under torture, and millions lost their lives. This fate was also that of many who, like me, were deported to Germany and forced to work for the Nazis. Sixty thousand of us died, victims of illnesses or bombings or even execution because of acts of resistance. Three hundred were assassinated on Good Friday 1945 by the Gestapo, in the forest clearing of the Bittermark in Dortmund.

WE MUST NEVER FORGET!

Elie and his wife, Solange, at a *Gasthof* behind the Möhnetal Dam, June 5, 2002.

Elie in front of the
Möhnetal Dam,
June 5, 2002.

Epilogue

In May 2000, at an exposition in the city of Dortmund,[1] Elie met Monsignor Charles Molette, who was there as the featured speaker in his function as president of the Association of Archivists of the Church in France—an association that he had founded in 1973—as well as a reknowned historian of the Church. Mollette, the son of a Jewish family, was born in Breslau in 1918. However, he converted to the Catholic Church and was ordained in 1943 in Paris. During the war, he was involved with the Mission Saint Paul, a church organization that sent French priests and seminarists to Nazi Germany to minister to the spiritual needs of the forced laborers of the STO. These priests and seminarists operated clandestinely at great risks to themselves, for a Nazi decree, dated December 3, 1943, called for the persecution of the activities of the Action Catholique Française among the *Zivilarbeiter* in the Reich.[2] In fact, it has been found that fifty Frenchmen from the STO were killed by the Nazis because of their faith.[3] They were not only priests but also seminarists, members of the JOC (to which Elie belonged), and even scouts.[4] These men have now been declared martyrs of the church, and Monsignor Mollette worked for their beatification until his death in 2013.

Sometime in 2005, Elie offered him a copy of the first edition of his *Mémoires*, and Monsignor Molette sent him an enthusiastic letter about it. The letter is published as the last page of the second edition of the book. Its letter head is in Latin and says: *Dioecesium Galliee Canonizationie Quinquaginta Servorum Dei Sacerdotum, Religiosorum, Clericorum necnon Laicorum Invenum in odium Fidel, uti fertar, aa. 1943-1945 interfectorum.*[5]

Postulator-general[6]   11, rue Férou, Paris 75006
                                         June 7, 2005
Dear Friend,

It is in one sitting that I have just read your testimony. These memories, which you had the excellent idea to put down on paper, are certainly important: These pages, full of life, are precious because of their accent of truth.

You did right to have given them the title that you have chosen with just cause. Yes, these are truly the "Memoirs of a *Jociste Déporté du Travail*." And these pages do show the "spiritual resistance," which was yours, as you lived it in 1943–1945, in the midst of so many horrors deliberately perpetrated, with also some sparks of humanity, solidarity, and friendship. Your faith too made you recognize signs of God in your own life as well as the relief of His Church.

These pages are certainly important for the truth of history. Thank you for having allowed me to read them. In these days of the 60th anniversary of the end of the nightmare, I can only formulate a wish: May this publication contribute to bringing attention to the nobility of man even when he is held up to ridicule.

With all my best wishes for you and your intentions. God bless you!
Signed:
Monsignor Charles Mollette

The French first and second editions of Elie's book were introduced by two forewords. The first was written by Elisabeth and Dieter Tillmann of Dortmund, Germany. These two academics and researchers have been particularly interested in the experiences of forced laborers in Germany during World War II, especially of those of religious faith, principally Catholics.

In the 1990s, Elisabeth Tillmann was writing a book on the history of the Catholic Church. When she reached the period of World War II, she looked for original sources to complete her work. Thus in 1994, she published a personal advertisement in a newspaper[7] whose readership was mostly former *Déportés du Travail*. She sought testimonials from forced laborers who had been sent to the camp of Loh near Dortmund.

Working for the Diocese of Paderborn, she also asked for the memories of those who had known a French priest by the name of Louis Gall. Although Elie had never been sent to the camp of Loh, he had been sent to several camps of the Todt Organization around Dortmund, and he had come to know Father Louis Gall, who had been a professor of philosophy at the Seminary of Soissons before the war.[8] Thus, Elie decided to answer the ad and came in contact with Mrs. Tillmann in 1994, first through letters and then in person, when the Tillmanns visited his home.

The following year, Elisabeth Tillmann wrote a bilingual book, in German and French, that was published by the Katholisches Bildungswerk der Dortmunder Dekanate, or the Catholic Educational Association of the Dortmund Deanery. The English translation of the title is *Destination Dortmund at the Service of the Third Reich: The Destiny of French Workers of the STO in the Camp of Loh, 1943–1945*.[9] Elie, who has always been a devout Catholic, is cited in many places in this book.

In their foreword to *Mémoires d'un Jociste*, the Tillmans wrote the following:

> We have rejected our scruples about the use of the term *"Déportés du Travail"* (knowing that this title is greatly disputed in France; we wanted to propose STO; but no!) Since this expression reflects historical truth, you need to use [in your book title] *"Déportés du Travail."*[10]
>
> In Germany, nobody understands why you were forbidden to use this designation. We authorize you to cite our opinion in a foreword if you want to.

Dear Elie, we are sure you know how much we regret all that you experienced in Germany during this sinister period of our history; how much we admire your Christian faith and the steadfastness with which you defended it during your captivity; and how much we are grateful to you for your friendship and for all you have done—and still do—for the reconciliation between our two peoples and for the Franco-German friendship.

Elisabeth and Dieter Tillmann, Dortmund (Germany)

Elisabeth Tillmann's work resulted in several articles and books on the subject of forced labor in wartime Germany, which were published in Germany. Some stressed the Catholic opposition to the Nazi regime, or "spiritual resistance," as Elie calls it. One book in particular, *Zwang und Zuwendung, Katholische Kirche und Zwangsarbeit im Ruhrgebiet*,[11] depicts, among other things, the role of the French Catholic Church's ministry to the French forced laborers. One chapter, written by Dieter Tillmann, devotes twenty pages to Elie's experience. Another chapter, written by Elisabeth, describes Father Louis Gall's ministry in wartime Germany.

The second foreword to the French editions of Elie's book was written by Roger Jaillot, a ceramic plant worker, a native of Decize (where Elie settled after the war) who also was sent to forced labor in Germany in 1944, after a police raid of an illegal dance organized to celebrate the coming of age of the young men of the class of 1944.[12] Here is what Mr. Jaillot wrote:

2005, the sixtieth anniversary of the liberation of [various German] camps, including those of *Déportés du Travail*.

A half century of negotiations to take back a title recognized by a decree, dated August 17, 1945, of the provisional government presided by General de Gaulle. This decree was signed by General de Gaulle and his ministers—Fresnay, Teitgen, Bidault, Tixier, Diethelm, Soustelle. [The decree was] rescinded later at the request of our opponents, and we were rebaptized "Victims and Survivors of Nazi Forced Labor Camps," without any form of legal proceedings.

This behavior and acts of all political groups during a half century prompted Elie Poulard to write an additional testimony of our living conditions during this sad period of Nazi slavery. To preserve the memory of an historical truth.[13]

Roger Jaillot, author from Burgundy
Victim of the Decize raid of February 6, 1944

As is quite evident, these two forewords as well as the letter from Monsignor Charles Mollette make reference to the title of *Déportés du Travail* and the controversy over it. This controversy has never ended and is likely to never be resolved before the last surviving *Déporté du Travail* has passed on. Thus, it seems fitting to conclude this book with an overview of this controversy. This is the subject of the following Appendix.

Appendix
A Dispute over a Title

From the time of the liberation of France in the summer of 1944 until the Constitution of the Fourth Republic was ratified in 1946, the country had a provisional government under the leadership of General Charles de Gaulle. After the end of the hostilities in Europe in May 1945, this government created a Ministère des Prisoniers, Déportés et Réfugiés, or Ministry of Prisoners, Deportees, and Refugees, to prepare for the return from Germany of hundreds of thousands of French citizens who had been sent there as prisoners of war, as political prisoners, for racial reasons, or as forced laborers. On August 14, 1945, the provisional government enacted a decree that instructed this ministry to publish all information it could collect about the conditions of the capture or arrest, internment in France, deportation, captivity, liberation, and repatriation of prisoners of war, deported and imprisoned persons, and finally of the *Déportés du Travail*.[1] The ministry was also instructed to put together three commissions or committees, one for each category of people mentioned above, to perform that task. The members of each commission were to be chosen by the ministry. The third, entitled La commission des Déportés du Travail, "was to be composed of a representative from each territorial [German] district (*Gau*)." This August 15, 1945, decree of the French provisional government was signed by Charles de Gaulle and five of his ministers and the keeper of the seals.

All those who had been sent to forced labor in Germany by the Vichy government concluded that this decree conferred on them the title of *Déportés du Travail.* In fact, it seems that this was not officially the case. Nevertheless, in 1945, a Fédération Nationale des Déportés du Travail[2] was created, which grouped together departmental associations. Thus, in each department into which France is administratively divided, an Association Départementale des Déportés du Travail was created. Each association was divided into sections in different cities and towns. Elie joined the section of Decize of the Nièvre departmental association, and took on a leadership role, becoming its president in the 1980s.

In 1948, however, the French Parliament passed two laws on August 6 and September 9 that gave the title of *Déportés* only to those who had been forcibly sent to a Nazi concentration camp or a prison.[3] Why these laws were passed is not clear.

One probable reason was that those who were sent to forced labor in Germany under the Vichy government's law of the Service Obligatoire du Travail (STO) were not put on the same level as those who had joined the Résistance or those who had been sent to concentration camps. The STOs, as they also were called, were considered suspect. Many questioned whether they had really been forced to leave for Germany. As the magazine *L'Histoire,* in a special edition, put it:

> Like many, they had suffered from hunger, from the cold, and had been under terrible bombardments. But, insofar as they had worked for Germany, received a salary, and retained a semblance of freedom even though their living conditions had remained difficult, did they not implicitly contribute to reinforce the enemy? . . . Certain accusers . . . treated them as German auxiliaries, even indeed as collaborators.[4]

Thus, those of the STO found themselves with an ambiguous status.

Still, there were some French politicians who did argue in favor of the title of *Déportés du Travail.* In 1950, the French National Assembly approved a bill on second reading that maintained the term *Déportés* for those "requisitioned for obligatory work in

Germany."[5] But the Senate did not vote in favor of that bill. Moreover, the following year that same assembly enacted a law on the status "of persons compelled to work in enemy territory, in foreign territory occupied by the enemy, or in French territory annexed by the enemy." As the newspaper *Le Monde* reported: "The word *Déporté* had disappeared."[6]

Because the Fédération Nationale des Déportés du Travail was sued over its use of the word *Déporté* by associations of people who had been deported to Nazi Germany for other reasons than the STO, it changed its title in 1979 to Fédération Nationale des Victimes Rescapées des Camps Nazis du Travail Forcé, or National Federation of Surviving Victims of Nazi Forced Labor Camps. Once again, the word *Déporté* had disappeared.

The departmental associations and their sections, however, continued to use the word. For this reason the associations of the departments of Tarn, Tarn-et-Garonne, and Lot-et-Garonne were sued in 1989 by the Association Départementale de Lot-et-Garonne des Déportés, Internés et Familles des Disparus, or Lot-et-Garonne Departmental Association of Deported, Internees, and Families of Those Who Had Disappeared. The suit ended up at the Court of Appeals of Toulouse, which ruled for the defendants. In its opinion, the Court argued that in the course of time, the word *Déporté* used by itself was understood by people to refer to persons who had been sent to Nazi concentration camps and prisons. When the word was qualified by *du travail*, the distinction was made clear. Furthermore, the Court stated that the use of the phrase *Déportés du Travail* in the title of an association was not against the law. Thus, the judges found the suit without merit.[7]

This decision could have concluded the controversy, but it did not. In 1992, the case was appealed to the highest French court, the Cour de Cassation.[8] During the hearing in front of the Court, harsh words were used, particularly by the lawyer for the litigants, Jacques Boré. Here is an excerpt from his plea:

> We must not confuse purgatory with hell. . . . Of the 600,000 requisitioned by the STO, 90 percent came back to a normal life after the end of the hostilities, whereas 80 percent of the

Déportés died. . . . It is the procession of all those who wore the striped costume of the concentration camps that comes today to ask you for the honor of not been mistaken for those who, after the call of Pierre Laval, went to build tanks in Germany.[9]

The lawyer for the defendants was Paul-François Rysiger. In answer to his adversary's vehement plea, he accused Boré of having "manhandled history." Rysiger then proceeded to make a review of the history of French forced labor in Germany. He stated that the words *Déportés du Travail* were uttered all the time during the war, that even the famous Résistant Jean Moulin had used the term "deportation" in a telegram referring to the STO. Rysiger concluded that the whole issue was a "nasty quarrel," and added: "It is unfortunate that fifty years after the war, we tear each other apart, we have this suit, and that we say: I suffered more than you; I have a right to this and not you."[10]

The Court ruled in favor of the litigants, basing its decision on the 1950 law, mentioned earlier, forbidding the words "deportation" or *Déportés* from the title of associations of persons sent to Germany by the STO. However, the presiding magistrate was unhappy with this decision, for he stated: "If times have changed, if the passing of time leads to another vision of this problem, which remains, alas, as a wound not healed, let us refer [the issue] to the Parliament."[11] As if in a parting gesture, the French government, on October 6, 2008, issued a decree declaring those who had been sent to Germany under the STO as "victims of forced labor in Nazi Germany."

It was after this decision of the Cour de Cassation that the newspaper *Le D.T.* changed its name to the *Proscrit* (the *Outlaw*). However, most associations of former STOs continued to use the title of *Déportés du Travail* as long as they were not sued. This was the case of the Nièvre association and its Decize section (to which Elie belonged) until it was dissolved in 2009 after the loss of most of its members.

⊸ As a conclusion to this controversy, it must be said that it happened only in France, not in Belgium, not in Holland, not in Poland, nor anywhere else in Europe. One might wonder what the events related above tell us about the French, a people steeped in René Descartes' philosophy.

All those young Frenchmen who were sent to forced labor in Germany by the Vichy government were clearly deported from their home country. There is no reason to call them anything other than:

DÉPORTÉS DU TRAVAIL.

Notes

1. Members of the French national police are called *gendarmes*.
2. The *Certificat d'Etudes* is a diploma obtained by passing a series of tests at the end of elementary school. In those days, relatively few French adolescents, especially from the working class, went on to the equivalent of high school. To be able to move on to secondary education, a day-long exam had to be successfully passed by children who were between ten and twelve years old. The vast majority of pupils remained in elementary school until age fourteen.
3. *Solfège* is the name the French give to the method of teaching the rudiments of music.
4. *La Garde Républicaine* is a military unit that provides security for the French president of the Republic. Its brass band often plays on horseback in parades.

1. Required Work Service. This law was promulgated on February 16, 1943, actually reinforcing a previous law passed on September 4, 1942.
2. Departmental Association of the Deportees for Work from the Nièvre. The title *Déportés du Travail* is rather difficult to succinctly translate into English. See the appendix for further information.
3. The members of the JOC were known as *Jocistes*.
4. Robert O. Paxton, *Vichy France: Old Guard and New Order, 1940–1944* (New York: Alfred A. Knopf, 1972), 366.

5. Robert O. Paxton, *La France de Vichy, 1940–1944*, trans. by Claude Bertrand (Paris: Edition du Seuil, 1997), 11.

6. Ibid., 14.

7. Paxton, *Vichy France*, 366.

8. Jean-Pierre Vittori, *Eux, Les STO* (Paris: Messidor/Temps Actuels, 1982), 9.

9. Ibid., 10. This expression cannot be translated literally. It means "there is nothing."

10. See Roger Jaillot, *Le Bal de la Classe — 6 février 1944 — de Decize . . . à Stuttgart . . . Nuremberg . . . Würtzburg.* (La Charité-sur-Loire: Delayance, 1985).

11. Ibid., 127.

12. See ibid., 206.

13. Best translated as "the truth of the matter."

14. Jacques Evrard, *La Déportation des Travailleurs Français dans le IIIe Reich* (Paris: Fayard, 1972), 9.

15. Ibid., 259.

16. Ibid., 441.

17. Ibid.

One   Still Free

1. *Patronage* also refers in France to a place that might include a large playground as well as a theater besides some other buildings. In those days, a Catholic priest would live on the premises.

2. A "fifth column" refers to a group of people who clandestinely undermine a larger group from within. The term originated in 1936 during the Spanish Civil War of 1936–39.

3. The root word for *paillons* is *paille*, which means straw. The *paillons* were cylinders made out of straw that were meant to protect the Champagne bottles in their wooden delivery boxes.

Two   The Real War and the Exodus

1. At the time of universal conscription in the army, Frenchmen were categorized by the year of their twentieth birthday. This was called their "class," and they would enter the military the following year. For Elie, this would have been 1941. Still today, in France, when people say to each other that they are of the same class, they mean that they were born in the same year.

2. In those days, the barber of Mareuil cut hair on Sunday mornings.

3. The Ponts et Chaussées is the name of the French agency that builds and maintains bridges and roads.

4. *Exode* is the French word for exodus, but it is also the word that the French use to describe the period of the war when thousands took to the roads to try to escape the German advance.

5. Troyes is a city some seventy miles straight south of Mareuil. The trip from Romilly would have normally taken forty-five minutes.

6. Pétain was a hero of World War I, and, in 1940, was given full powers by the French National Assembly to be the head of the government.

7. Listening to Radio London was strictly forbidden by the German occupying authorities. The good mayor was in fact concerned for the safety of Elie and the Chalon family.

Three   Back Home under German Occupation

1. The Messageries Hachette were press distributing services of the publishing company Hachette.

2. A *sou* at that time was a twentieth of a frank. Twenty *sous* was the price for cheap novels.

3. *Beautiful Stories of Courage*. This publication replaced the magazine *Cœurs Vaillants* (*Valiant Hearts*), which was banned by the Germans. This was the magazine of the Cœurs Vaillants, a Catholic youth organization similar to the Boy Scouts.

4. The Faux de Verzy is a forest notorious for its oaks that are twisted and not very high.

5. On Gabriel Favréaux, see Jean V. Poulard, *The Champagne Cellars of Mareuil: The Story of a Family and a Village, 1939–1948* (Montigny-le-Bretonneux: Yvelinedition, 2011), chaps. 6 and 7.

Four   In Bondage

1. Literally "relief," as in the relief of troops or as in the changing of the guard.

2. This Nazi organization bore the name of its founder, Fritz Todt, an expert in the construction of roads and tunnels. After Todt's death in a mysterious plane crash in February 1942, Albert Speer succeeded him as chief of this body, which was in charge of the construction of large projects, especially those of a military nature.

3. Each department of France is typically divided into several administrative districts: one *préfecture* and from two to six *sous-préfectures*. The department of the Marne has four *sous-préfectures*.

4. The word *maquis* literally is the name of a bush that grows especially in Corsica. During the war, the word referred to where the French Résistance took refuge, usually in forests. Someone who joined the Résistance became known as a *maquisard*.

5. It is really impossible to find a good English translation for this title that would make sense. Literally it means "the king of pliers." Apparently, that fellow could use his hands like cutting pliers.

6. The Milice was a paramilitary force created by the Vichy government that helped the Germans fight the Résistance.

7. A pun is often impossible to translate, or at least it loses a lot in translation. In this case, Keufer, when pronounced by a Frenchman, sounds like the French phrase which means "What to do?" Förster, in the same way, sounds like the French phrase meaning "We must be quiet." The French version of this story put it this way: "Keufer puisqu'il Förster?" ("Que faire puisqu'il faut se taire?").

8. Négus was the name given to the king of Ethiopia. Vercingétorix was a Gaulish chieftain, supposedly with a great mustache, who fought Julius Caesar and lost. Staviski was a bank director involved in an embezzling scandal in 1933 in Bayonne, France.

Five   Deported to Germany

1. Those who were deported under the STO law often referred to themselves as "STO."

2. There has been a controversy in France over the term "deportation," as well as the word *déporté*. Many people have argued that the "title" of *déporté* should not be applied to those who went to Germany under the STO law, but should only be applied to those who ended up in concentration camps.

3. Pierre Tantet had been a captain in the French army. In November 1943, he was hunted down by the Gestapo, but he escaped to hide in Paris. After the liberation of Mareuil, he was elected mayor of the village. For more on Tantet, see Poulard, *The Champagne Cellars of Mareuil*.

4. Pierre Laval was prime minister to Pétain and was instrumental in creating the STO.

Six   Work at the Möhnetal Dam

1. Charleroi is a city in Belgium in the middle of a coal-mining region. Torremans was a Walloon, a French-speaking Belgian.

2. Pietro Badoglio was a commander of Italian fascist troops under Benito Mussolini. However, when Mussolini was arrested on July 24, 1943, Badoglio became prime minister and joined the side of the Allies.

3. Léon Blum was three times prime minister of France. He was a leader of the French Socialist Party, known by its French initials, SFIO. He struggled against the fascists and the communists. In 1943, as a Jew, he was deported to the concentration camp of Buchenwald and later to Dachau. However, he survived the war and died in 1950. The German's phrase means: "Léon Blum, nice!"

4. Elie was named after his uncle who was killed in 1914 in eastern France during World War I.

Seven   Living Conditions at the Dam

1. The Morvan is the region of central France around where Elie was born. Villars and Saint-Honoré-les-Bains are part of it.

2. The Crédit Lyonnais is one of France's largest banks, if not the largest. It was nationalized in 1945.

Eight   Hagen-in-Westfalen and Its Camps

1. An *Ausweiss* is a pass. OT, of course, stands for Organization Todt.

2. It is interesting to note that Elie, who had a fantastic memory for names, does not mention the name of this fellow.

3. As noted in the author's preface, JOC stands for Jeunesse Ouvrière Catholique, an organization of the church to keep young people in their faith after they started to work.

Nine   Work at the *Telegraphenamt* of Hagen

1. "Please, do not sing!" Actually the English translation does not give the real nuance of the German phrase. The conductor, in fact, was saying: "It is really not an appropriate time to sing!"

2. S.A. stands for *Sturmabteilung*. This was the first paramilitary force of the Nazi party. The people in it wore a brown uniform and were called "brown shirts."

Ten   Life at the Boeler Heide Camp

1. *Casse croûte* were thick rectangular biscuits that were served as snacks. The name is best translated as "a bite to eat."
2. The Nièvre department is in central France where Saint-Honoré-les-Bains is located.

Eleven   Dortmund-South Work Site

1. *Oiseaux* literally means birds. I do not know why that word was used to name the containers.

Twelve   Dortmund *Hauptbahnof* after October 6, 1944

1. It was the Royal Canadian Air Force that bombed Dortmund that day.
2. The men in striped clothing must have come from a concentration camp.

Fourteen   On the Ruhr

1. A *Gauleiter* was a leader of a regional branch of the Nazi party.
2. Jean Fonse, when pronounced together in French, sounds like: "I sink," or "I push something, into something else," or "Jean goes fast."

Fifteen   In Railroad Yards Still and Again

1. It is difficult to translate this expression. It means: "You look terrible!" However, the essence is lost in translation.
2. The literal translation of Volkssturm is "Storm of the People." It was a sort of people's army, a drafted national militia organized in November 1944.

Sixteen   My Last Week as a Slave

1. The Ruhr River is very wide in that area because of a dam, and thus it was referred to as a lake.
2. This is a German military rank equivalent to that of sergeant.

Epilogue

1. The exposition about French forced laborers in Nazi Germany was entitled "Zum 'Reicheinsatz' nach Dortmund — Französische Zwangsarbeiter im Lager Loh, 1943–1945," and was organized by Elisabeth Tillmann.
2. The Nazis called this religious activity *Die grosse Sache,* "the big thing."
3. The list of these men is in the editor's possession. The list actually contained fifty-one names: twenty *Jocistes,* nine priests, four seminarists, fourteen scouts, and four listed as O.F.M. The extra name is of a *Jociste* already beatified: Marcel Callo, who was from the city of Rennes in Brittany, was STO in Thuringia and died in the concentration camp of Mauthausen.
4. In France, the Catholic Church has always been very involved with the scouting movement, and thus French scouts have tended to be highly religious.
5. The letterhead refers to the French appeal for the beatification of the fifty martyrs.
6. A postulator is a person who leads the process to canonize or beatify someone in the Roman Catholic Church.
7. This newspaper, called *Le D.T.,* was published by the Fédération nationale des victimes et rescapés des camps Nazis du travail forcé. *Le D.T.* stands for the *Déporté du Travail.* This newspaper was renamed *Le Proscrit* around 1992.
8. Elie mentions Father Louis Gall several times in the chapters above.
9. Elisabeth Tillmann, *Destination Dortmund au service du IIIe Reich: Le destin des travailleus français du STO au camp Loh, 1943–1945* (Dortmund: Katholisches Bildungswerk der Dortmunder Dekanate, 1995).
10. As mentioned earlier, the translation of this phrase, "Deported Workers," does not seem to fit well in the text, for it is a purely French title, which however has found opposition against its use by those who were sent to Nazi concentration camps and who called themselves simply *Déportés.* See the appendix in this volume.

11. Baldur Hermans, ed., *Zwang und Zuwendung: Katholische Kirche und Zwangsarbeit im Ruhrgebiet* [*Force and Care: The Catholic Church and Forced Labor in the Ruhr Region*] (Bochum: Verlag Kamp, 2003).

12. Roger Jaillot wrote about the raid and his experience in Germany. See Roger Jaillot, *Le Bal de la Classe — 6 février 1944 — de Decize . . . à Stuttgart . . . Nuremberg . . . Würtzburg* (La Charité-sur-Loire: Impressions Delayance, 1985).

13. According to Elie Poulard, Roger Jaillot is not quite correct in his statement about the title *Déportés du Travail*. The decree mentioned did not officially recognize that title.

Appendix

1. See *Journal Officiel de la République Française*, August 17, 1945.

2. The name is best translated not literally but as National Federation of Those Deported [to Germany] for Forced Labor.

3. The August 6, 1948, law was entitled "Statut Définitif des Déportés et Internés de la Résistance," or "Definitive Status of the Deported and Internees of the Resistance." The September 9 law went further by creating a medal for such people, the Médaille de la Déportation et de l'Internement Politique.

4. *L'Histoire*, no. 80, pp. 105–6. This magazine does not show a date of publication. This special edition is entitled *Résistants et Collaborateurs: Les Français dans les années noires*.

5. See *Journal Officiel de la République Française*, August 4, 1950.

6. *Le Monde*, February 4, 1992.

7. See *Le D.T.*, no. 271, December 1989.

8. While this is the highest French court, it is not comparable to the United States Supreme Court. It is composed of a large number of magistrates divided into several chambers, each specializing in a certain type of law. This court, unlike the U.S. Supreme Court, does not have the option to choose the cases it will hear. All must be heard. And the court does not have the power of judicial review.

9. Quoted in *Le Monde*, February 4, 1992.

10. Ibid.

11. Ibid.

Bibliography

Books

Evrard, Jacques. *La Déportation des Travailleurs Français dans le IIIe Reich*. Paris: Fayard, 1972.

Fédération Nationale des Victimes et Rescapés des camps nazis du travail forcé. *Un livre blanc sur une période noire*. Tours: Imprimerie S.A.T.R., 1987.

Hermans, Baldur, ed. *Zwang und Zuwendung, Katholische Kirche und Zwangsarbeit im Ruhrgebiet*. Bochum: Verlag Kamp, 2003.

Jaillot, Roger, *Le Bal de la Classe—6 février 1944—de Decize . . . à Stuttgart . . . Nuremberg . . . Würtzburg*. La Charité-sur-Loire: Impressions Delayance, 1985.

———. *La vérité sur les départs des travailleurs français en Allemagne*. Decize: Imprimerie Barlerin, 2001.

———. *Le temps de la déportation du travail, 1942–1945*. Decize: Imprimerie Barlerin, 2001.

———. *L'après-guerre et des combats d'octogénaires*. Decize: Imprimerie Barlerin, 2006.

La main-d'œuvre française exploitée par le IIIe Reich. Colloque International (13-14-15 décembre 2001) au Mémorial de la Paix à Caen. Decize: Imprimerie Barlerin, 2001.

Paxton, Robert O. *Vichy France: Old Guard and New Order, 1940–1944*. New York: Alfred A. Knopf, 1972.

———. *La France de Vichy, 1940–1944*. Translated by Claude Bertrand. Paris: Editions du Seuil, 1997.

Poulard, Jean V. *The Champagne Cellars of Mareuil: The Story of a Family and of a Village, 1939–1948*. Montigny-le-Bretonneux: Yvelinedition, 2011.

Tillmann, Elisabeth. *Destination Dortmund au service du IIIe Reich: Le destin des travailleurs français du STO au camp Loh, 1943–1945.* Dortmund: Katholisches Bildungswerk der Dortmunder Dekanate, 1995.

Vittori, Jean-Pierre. *Eux, les S.T.O.* Paris: Messidor/Temps Actuels, 1982.

Newspapers and Magazines

Journal Officiel de la République Française, August 17, 1945.

Journal Officiel de la République Française, August 4, 1950.

Le D. T., no. 271, December 1989.

Le Proscrit.

Le Monde, February 4, 1992.

L'Histoire, no. 80.

Elie Poulard lives in France.

Jean V. Poulard, his brother and translator,
is professor of political science at Indiana University Northwest.

Lightning Source UK Ltd.
Milton Keynes UK
UKHW022007230222
399141UK00003B/131